"When it comes to creating great BBQ flavor, Ray's book delivers. His straightforward approach to creating award-winning BBQ sauces makes this book a great addition to anyone's cookbook collection."

—JUNIOR URIAS, pitmaster of Up In Smoke BBQ

"Finally, a BBQ sauce master who boldly shares his most awarded sauce recipes. If you want to learn the secrets to making great BBQ sauces, as well as some simply scrumptious ways to use them, then you need this book!"

— KIM PERRY, pitmaster of Behind BBQ, winner of *American Grilled*

"I can't wait to get my hands on this cookbook and make some of Ray's favorite BBQ dishes."

—REBECKA EVANS, creator of At Home with Rebecka, 2017 Bacon World Champion

"Ray is a talented chef and an aficionado of barbecue. He is dedicated to his craft, and only delivers the best."

—MATTHEW DEATON, pitmaster, chef at FoodE restaurant

"We knew we picked a winner when Ray Sheehan was on our show. Not only did he make good tv but also great BBQ! His award-winning sauces are still being used in our TV kitchen today!"

—BRYAN SCOFIELD, Emmy-award-winning anchor and co-host at *PA Live!* WBRE-TV NBC

Award-Winning
BBQ SAUCES
AND HOW TO USE THEM

The SECRET INGREDIENT TO
NEXT-LEVEL SMOKING

RAY SHEEHAN

CERTIFIED KANSAS CITY BARBEQUE SOCIETY JUDGE

**WICKLOW COUNTY COUNCIL
LIBRARY SERVICE**

PAGE STREET
PUBLISHING CO.

PAGE STREET
PUBLISHING CO.

First published in 2020 by

Page Street Publishing Co.

27 Congress Street, Suite 105

Salem, MA 01970

www.pagestreetpublishing.com

Distributed by Macmillan, sales in Canada by The Canadian Manda Group.

24 23 22 21 20   1 2 3 4 5

ISBN-13: 978-1-64567-005-6

ISBN-10: 1-64567-005-8

Library of Congress Control Number: 2019906548

Cover and book design by Rosie Stewart for Page Street Publishing Co.

Photography by Ken Goodman

Printed and bound in China

Page Street Publishing protects our planet by donating to nonprofits like The Trustees, which focuses on local land conservation.

For my son, Raymond.

You are the joy of my life, the source of my dearest memories and the inspiration for all my achievements. I am so very proud of the young man that you are becoming, and I will forever cherish the bond that we have created while cooking barbecue together.

I LOVE YOU.

Contents

Foreword

Ray and I met back in 2014 at a competition-style pork and brisket class I was teaching at my home in Pennsylvania. He had not been exposed to competition barbecue before that day, but he stood out as being experienced in the culinary world and seemed very eager to learn as much as he could about the art and science of real barbecue. I do believe that day something inside him clicked and told him one day he would become a "BBQ Buddha."

Once Ray gained some knowledge and experience with cooking large cuts of meat properly on the pit, his creative mind went to work on how he could develop his own flavor profiles to accompany these wonderfully tender morsels. He spent countless hours in the kitchen and at the grill, testing and tweaking sauces and rubs to get that perfect balance of flavors we all strive for. The wonderful thing about testing food products is the fact that there are always neighbors, friends and family who are more than willing to give you their opinions on the potential final product as long as they are fed well.

Soon after he perfected his sauces and rubs, when he met up with some folks who were interested in starting a BBQ competition team in the mid-Atlantic region, he joined in, introduced them to his products and the awards started trickling in weekend after weekend.

Ray has earned several top awards in the pork, ribs and brisket categories. He has won several chili and bacon competitions over the years as well. He and his team took top 10 honors at the Boo-B-Que BBQ contest in Rehoboth Beach, Delaware, which had a field of over 60 championship teams and has grown to be one of the largest Kansas City Barbeque Society events on the East Coast. He has even competed successfully in the World Food Championships in Orange Beach, Alabama.

Although he has won many awards for cooking BBQ, where he really excels is in creating award-winning BBQ sauces. Ray's passion and persistence have won him an impressive collection of top honors in some of the largest, most prestigious sauce competitions in the world.

Ray and I grew up in similar families that were always having backyard gatherings around the open flames and smoke of the grill. The fascination of cooking meats over open coals while dashing them with spices and herbs inspired him to learn as much as he could about grilling, barbecue, seasonings and, best of all, the sauces that complement them.

This book is well thought out and fantastic to have by your side when you are ready to light the grill.

Ray's recipes deliver the flavor profiles you will need to create everything from classic sauces like Kansas City style and Memphis mop to some excitingly unique and wonderful flavors, such as cherry bourbon and tangy peach. The entrée recipes he uses in this book will tantalize your taste buds and have your guests coming back for more.

This isn't just another barbecue cookbook with the same ol', same ol' recipes. When a BBQ Guru recommends a BBQ Buddha, you may want to take his advice!

BOB TRUDNAK,

Pitmaster of the BBQ Guru Competition Team and Barbecue World Champion

Introduction

From a young age, I spent countless hours on my grandfather's farm, where he gifted me an appreciation for hard work and honest, good food. There were many days when he would prepare an entire meal over an open fire. I was mesmerized by the smell of the burning wood, the sound of the fire crackling and the anticipation of the finished meal. You can say that these moments ignited my passion and what has become a lifelong obsession with outdoor cooking.

I had a burning desire to learn all that I could about food, so much so that I went to the most highly regarded restaurant on the Jersey shore, which at the time was rated in *Gourmet* magazine's Top Tables, and convinced its chef-owner, Chris Mumford, to allow me to apprentice there. I would go to the restaurant, after working my regular job as a baker from four a.m. until noon, to receive hands-on training in a no-nonsense kitchen. It was an experience that I am grateful for to this day. I learned important knife skills, sauce making and how to develop my palate. I gained a much deeper respect for food and where it comes from. Chris was way ahead of his time. Equipped with a smoker out back and cultivating a 1.5-acre (6,000-km) organic garden, his restaurant, Mumford's Unique American Cuisine, was creating a farm-to-table dining experience over two decades ago.

This experience set me on a path to culinary school, where I learned the finer points of French cuisine. During and after my formal education, I worked in many facets of the food industry, holding every position from dishwasher up to chef, yet I was still restless.

As I grew older my fascination with barbecue cooking only intensified, and I experimented regularly with a charcoal grill. Then, one year on my birthday, my wife gifted me a smoker, and I was instantly hooked. Immediately, I began creating sauces and rubs to flavor the smoked meats that I had been carefully cooking for hours on end.

My sauce and rub creations were so well received at cookouts, family gatherings and even barbecue competitions that in 2015, I decided to make a go of it as a business and developed the BBQ Buddha brand.

I never could have dreamed where my barbecue journey would take me. I have competed head to head against some of the top pitmasters in the country and have gotten calls in such categories as chicken, ribs, pork, brisket, bacon and chili. However, none has been as gratifying as the accolades and awards that I have received for my BBQ sauces in some of the biggest national and international competitions. BBQ Buddha sauces have won top awards in such competitions as the American Royal "Best Sauce on the Planet" contest, the National Barbecue and Grilling Association's Awards of Excellence, the Scovie Awards, the World Hot Sauce Awards and the International Flavor Awards (the Flaves).

This wonderful BBQ adventure has become my life. I have my own line of BBQ sauces and rubs on grocery store shelves, teach outdoor cooking classes and compete on the pro barbecue circuit. What more could I ask for? You guessed it . . . this cookbook!

While creating award-winning BBQ sauces and rubs is certainly a passion of mine, I am driven by inspiring and teaching others how to grill, smoke and create their own delicious BBQ.

In this book, you will find the recipes for my most awarded sauce, BBQ Buddha's Memphis Mop BBQ Sauce (page 17), as well as my Kansas City BBQ Sauce (page 61). In fact, all the sauces shared within these pages have helped me earn numerous awards in barbecue and grilling competitions throughout the Northeast and beyond.

With 60 recipes, I will show you five ways to utilize each of the ten different BBQ sauces. Some may be classic techniques that you have always wanted to master, but you may not have even thought of others, such as how to incorporate these delicious BBQ sauces into nearly every meal, including breakfast!

So cook along with me, chapter by chapter, to discover the tastes and techniques that I use and take your grilling and smoking to the next level.

Use the recipes in this book as a blueprint. Mix and match the sauces in each and create your own unique flavor profile. Whatever combination that you decide on, you can't go wrong. These sauces, rubs, brines and marinades are the foundation of what great barbecue flavor is built on.

Ray Sheehan

Sauce Basics

MY SECRET INGREDIENT

When I first began creating BBQ sauces, I must have tried over 100 different recipe variations before I came up with "the one." After much trial and error, I began to realize that I had to first balance the key elements of sweet, sour, spicy and salty with my base. Only then could I layer the flavors with notes of spice and smoke, before adding my secret ingredient.

For this sauce, as well as all the other barbecue products that I have created, the secret ingredient was actually something that I did not put in the recipe. I left out all the artificial colors, flavors and preservatives that are typically found in commercially bottled sauces, opting instead to use only natural, premium ingredients.

The decision to leave out high-fructose corn syrup and flavor enhancers, such as monosodium glutamate, has paid off. When I chose to bottle the Memphis Mop BBQ Sauce (page 17) as one of my first products, it was because I loved its sweet and tangy flavor. As it turns out, I wasn't the only one that has loved its naturally great taste. This sauce has brought me more accolades than all my other products combined.

I believe that, when given the choice, most people will choose foods that contain no harmful additives. Rest assured that all the sauce recipes in this book are free of anything artificial and showcase only those ingredients that you would feel good about giving to your family.

BUILDING FLAVOR

Did you know that in some parts of the country, talking barbecue can be taken as seriously as talking about religion? It would appear that every region has its own version of what true barbecue is. While this has sparked many debates among barbecue enthusiasts, one thing is for sure: To build a great BBQ sauce, you must begin with the essentials.

Start with a good base—this is the foundation on which the sauce will be built. Here are some examples of common bases:

TOMATO—fresh tomatoes, canned tomatoes, tomato puree, tomato paste, ketchup

VINEGAR—distilled white, cider, balsamic, white wine, red wine, Champagne

MUSTARD—Dijon, yellow, spicy brown, hot, Creole

Balance the flavors by adding these key elements:

SWEET—cane sugar, brown sugar, honey, molasses, maple syrup, corn syrup, rice syrup, jams, jellies

SOUR—vinegar, lemon juice, mustard, tamarind, pickle juice

SPICY—chile peppers, ground black or white pepper, hot pepper sauce, cayenne pepper, red pepper flakes, horseradish, grated ginger

SALTY—kosher salt, sea salt, soy sauce, Asian fish sauce, hoisin sauce, Worcestershire sauce, anchovy paste, olives, capers

SAVORY—raw or cooked onion, onion powder, raw or cooked garlic, granulated garlic or garlic powder, garlic salt, celery seed, celery salt, chili powder, fresh or dried herbs

SPICES—Many BBQ sauces include a range of seasonings. Try mixing it up with your favorite combination of both sweet spices (such as allspice, anise seeds, cinnamon, cloves, ginger and nutmeg) and savory spices (such as coriander, cumin, dill seed, mustard seed, paprika, pepper and sage).

SMOKE—A great way to infuse your BBQ sauce with smoke flavor is by using smoked paprika. You can also add a few drops of natural liquid smoke.

SECRET INGREDIENTS—Here are some of my favorites: Chinese five-spice powder, black garlic, bourbon, pork fat, beef drippings, coffee, butter, vanilla extract, liquor, apple cider, dried porcini mushrooms, cherry juice and bacon. What's your secret ingredient?

WOOD TYPES

Although smoke is an integral part of the barbecue flavor profile, sometimes less is more. You want it to work harmoniously with the other components of your dish. It is best used in moderation, like a seasoning, such as salt or pepper.

Many different types of smoke wood are available. Here is a list of some of the most common varieties, their characteristics and suggested food pairings.

APPLE—Mild, slightly sweet, fruity smoke flavor. Great with pork and chicken.

SUGAR MAPLE—Sweet and mild flavor. Works well with poultry, pork and cheese.

HICKORY—Strong smoky flavor with a hint of bacon. Goes well with pork, ribs, wild game and beef.

CHERRY—Slightly sweet, fruity smoke flavor. Goes great with pork and poultry.

MESQUITE—Strong earthy flavor; use in moderation. Works well with beef.

PEACH—Milder and sweeter than hickory. Works well with chicken and pork.

PECAN—A milder version of hickory. Great with poultry, pork and beef.

The Sauce That Won
"BEST BBQ SAUCE IN THE WORLD"

While creating the recipe for this BBQ sauce in my home kitchen, I looked to Memphis for inspiration, as it is a city that takes great pride in its barbecue culture.

In Memphis, barbecue means pork, and most notably pork ribs. While smoke wood and charcoal are integral to the cooking process, the region is home to variations in rib preparation. Some cooks apply fragrant spice blends to the meat and prefer to serve them up dry, usually without sauce. Others will baste the ribs with sauce while they cook, building layers of flavor over time, and serve the ribs with an accompaniment of sauce.

Memphis-style BBQ sauce is known for its simplicity, although the specific ingredients will vary from cook to cook. It is usually made with tomatoes, vinegar, mustard and countless combinations of spices. It is generally thin, with a bit of a tang. It is not too sweet, too thick, too spicy and might not be too anything . . . except too good!

Drawing from my background in the natural food world, I created this recipe, and all my sauce recipes, to be health-minded. Although my sauces are not certified organic, they contain no artificial ingredients. I believe the numerous awards my sauces have received are a testament to the great flavor of natural ingredients.

This chapter pays homage to the Memphis BBQ sauce's classic pairing with pork, but I couldn't resist and just had to include my wife's amazing turkey burger. I think you'll be glad that I did.

This Memphis Mop BBQ Sauce is sweet, tangy and packed with flavor. The secret to its success is that it is well balanced. It's not overly sweet, nor is it too spicy. However, it has just the right combination of spices to give you a little kick at the end, leaving the flavors lingering on your palate and you wanting more.

I never could have imagined the accolades that this sauce would bring me. I had no idea that you could win awards for making BBQ sauce, never mind winning "Best BBQ Sauce in the World." At the Fifth Annual World Hot Sauce Awards that took place in Baton Rouge, Louisiana, we won both the Vinegar and Memphis BBQ Sauce categories outright to become the Barbecue Sauce Divisional Champion. What's more impressive is that the wins came against sauces from twelve different countries across fourteen categories.

MAKES ABOUT 3 CUPS (710 ML) SAUCE

Memphis Mop BBQ Sauce

2 cups (475 ml) ketchup, such as Simply Heinz

½ cup (88 g) prepared yellow mustard

½ cup (115 g) packed light brown sugar

½ cup (120 ml) water

¼ cup (60 ml) cider vinegar

3 tbsp (45 ml) Worcestershire sauce

1 tbsp (7 g) onion powder

1 tbsp (8 g) chili powder

1½ tsp (3 g) freshly ground black pepper

2 tsp (6 g) granulated garlic

½ tsp celery salt

½ tsp salt

1 tbsp (15 ml) natural hickory liquid smoke

In a medium-sized saucepan, combine all the ingredients, except the liquid smoke. Bring it to a gentle boil over medium heat, stirring to dissolve the sugar. Lower the heat to low and simmer until it's slightly thickened, 20 to 25 minutes, stirring occasionally. With a whisk, blend in the liquid smoke until it's incorporated. Let the sauce cool, transfer it to a jar and store it in the refrigerator for up to a month.

The secret to perfecting these Memphis-style ribs is all in the sauce. You must cook them undisturbed for the first 90 minutes to develop the crust, then you can begin adding layers of flavor by mopping them every 45 minutes or so. Memphis ribs do not get wrapped during the smoking process, so it is important to keep them moist as they cook.

MAKES 4 TO 6 SERVINGS

SLOW-SMOKED MEMPHIS-STYLE RIBS

MEMPHIS RIB RUB

½ cup (144 g) sea salt

¼ cup (60 g) turbinado sugar

¼ cup (60 g) light brown sugar

1 tbsp (7 g) paprika

1 tbsp (8 g) chili powder

1 tbsp (7 g) onion powder

1 tbsp (9 g) dry mustard

1½ tsp (5 g) granulated garlic

1 tsp dried thyme

1 tsp dried oregano

1 tsp freshly ground black pepper

1 tsp celery salt

1 tsp ground ginger

½ tsp ground coriander

½ tsp cayenne pepper

2 (2½-lb [1.1-kg]) slabs baby back ribs

¼ cup (44 g) prepared yellow mustard

Hickory or cherry wood

1¼ cups (300 ml) Memphis Mop BBQ Sauce (page 17), warmed, for brushing, plus ¼ cup (60 ml) reserved for final glaze

Wooden toothpick, for testing doneness

Prepare the rub: In a medium-sized bowl, stir together all the rub ingredients and set it aside. Leftover rub may be stored in an airtight container for up to 6 months.

Prepare a smoker to cook at 250°F (120°C).

Remove the membrane from the back of the ribs and trim away any excess fat. Apply a thin coat of mustard to each side. Dust with an even layer of the rib rub to both sides of the ribs. Let them sit for 30 minutes to let the rub set up. Once the cooker reaches temperature, add the wood and place the ribs in the smoker, meat side up. Cook for 1½ hours, mop with the BBQ sauce and continue to mop every 45 minutes.

At around the 4-hour mark, start checking the ribs for tenderness: The ribs are done when a toothpick inserted into the meat goes in and out easily and you can see the meat shrink from the bone by about ¼ inch (6 mm), about 5 hours total.

Slice the ribs individually and arrange them on a platter. Using a clean brush, give them a glaze of additional mop sauce and a light dusting of the rib rub before serving.

I am a big fan of brining, especially for leaner cuts of meat like pork chops. It helps keep the meat tender and moist as it cooks. Allow the beer brine to infuse overnight for the best flavor, then grill and brush the chops with the glaze during the last five minutes of cooking. Your taste buds will thank you!

MAKES 6 SERVINGS

Beer-Brined Pork Chops with Memphis Glaze

GARLIC RUB
6 cloves garlic, minced

2 tsp (12 g) salt

2 tsp (6 g) freshly ground black pepper

2 tsp (1 g) dried sage leaves

½ tsp dried thyme

BRINE
2 cups (475 ml) water

2 cups (475 ml) dark lager beer

¼ cup (75 g) coarse salt

¼ cup (60 g) dark brown sugar

¼ cup (85 g) molasses

6 bone-in center-cut pork chops, 1½" (4-cm) thick

Memphis Mop BBQ Sauce (page 17), warmed, for brushing

Prepare the garlic rub: In a small bowl, stir together the garlic, salt, pepper, sage and thyme and set it aside.

Prepare the brine: In a large bowl, mix together all the brine ingredients until the sugar and salt have dissolved.

Place the chops in a ziplock bag. Pour the brine over the chops and seal the bag; refrigerate them for 8 hours or up to overnight, turning occasionally. Remove the chops from the bag and discard the brine. Pat the chops dry with paper towels and season them with the garlic rub.

Set up a charcoal grill for 2-zone cooking: Light a charcoal chimney, and when the edges of the charcoal at the top of the chimney begin to ash over, dump the pile of hot coals onto 1 side of the grill to form your hot side (direct cooking), leaving the other side empty to form your cool side (indirect cooking), forming 2 zones.

Once the charcoal is ready, place the chops on the cooking grate on the direct heat zone. Cook for about 4 minutes. Flip the chops and cook for 4 minutes more. Move the pork to the indirect-heat zone, brush them with the BBQ sauce and place the lid back on the grill. Cook until the chops have an internal temperature of 145 to 150°F (63 to 66°C), 5 to 6 minutes.

Remove the glazed chops from the grill and let them rest for about 10 minutes before serving.

My wife first started making these burgers to bring along on one of our camping trips, and now they are a staple at all our campfire cookouts. She starts by blending the BBQ sauce directly into the meat and forming them into patties before we hit the road, allowing the flavors plenty of time to come together. Here, I paired it with a sweet and spicy slaw that adds a nice crunch and contrast to the tender burger meat.

MAKES 4 SERVINGS

BBQ-Infused Turkey Burgers with Apple Jalapeño Slaw

APPLE JALAPEÑO SLAW

½ cup (115 g) mayonnaise

2 tbsp (30 g) sour cream

1 tbsp (11 g) Dijon mustard

1 tbsp (15 ml) cider vinegar

1 tbsp (13 g) sugar

1 tbsp (15 ml) fresh lemon juice

1 (1-lb [455-g]) package coleslaw mix

2 scallions, thinly sliced

1 Gala apple, peeled and thinly sliced

1 jalapeño pepper, seeded and diced

Salt and freshly ground black pepper

BURGERS

¼ cup (60 ml) Memphis Mop BBQ Sauce (page 17), divided

2 tbsp (14 g) dried bread crumbs

¾ tsp chili powder

½ tsp granulated garlic

½ tsp onion powder

¼ tsp salt

1 lb (455 g) ground turkey, 94% lean

TO SERVE

4 tbsp (56 g) unsalted butter, at room temperature

4 hamburger buns

4 thick slices tomato

4 green leaf lettuce leaves

4 tbsp (60 ml) Memphis Mop BBQ Sauce (page 17)

In a medium-sized bowl, combine the mayonnaise, sour cream, mustard, vinegar, sugar and lemon juice. Add the coleslaw mix, scallions, apple and jalapeño and mix well. Season with salt and black pepper to taste. Refrigerate the slaw until ready to use.

(Continued)

BBQ-Infused Turkey Burgers with Apple Jalapeño Slaw (Continued)

Prepare the burger patties: In a medium-sized bowl, combine half of the BBQ sauce with the bread crumbs, chili powder, granulated garlic, onion powder, salt and ground turkey. Divide the turkey mixture into 4 equal portions, shaping each into a 1½-inch (4-cm)-thick patty. Refrigerate them for 30 minutes, or until you're ready to cook.

Set up a charcoal grill for 2-zone cooking. Light a charcoal chimney, and when the edges of the charcoal at the top of the chimney begin to ash over, dump the pile of hot coals onto 1 side of the grill to form your hot side (direct cooking), leaving the other side empty to form your cool side (indirect cooking), forming 2 zones.

Once the charcoal is ready, place the burgers on the grate over the hot coals and cook for about 3 minutes. Flip the burgers and cook for another 3 minutes. Move the burgers to the indirect heat zone and baste them with the remaining BBQ sauce. Place the lid on the grill and cook until the burgers reach an internal temperature of 165°F (74°C), about 8 minutes.

While the burgers are cooking, butter the interior side of the buns with 1 tablespoon (14 g) of butter per bun and set them aside until you are ready to toast them.

Transfer the cooked burgers to a plate and tent them with foil to rest.

Place the buns, buttered side down, on the grate over the hot coals for 30 to 45 seconds to toast, keeping an eye on them so they don't burn.

To build your burger, layer the bottom half of each bun with a tomato slice, a burger patty, more BBQ sauce, a lettuce leaf and apple jalapeño slaw, then add a toasted bun top.

This wildly popular dish was created by Dan Starin at Spice It Up, a specialty grocery store and sandwich shop in Beach Haven, New Jersey. Dan's original "Pig Cone" is a waffle cone that is stuffed with layers of pulled pork that has been coated in Memphis Mop BBQ Sauce (page 17) and a creamy slaw. Just before serving, he tops it with a drizzle of smoked maple syrup.

Although it was a challenge to improve on something already so delicious, I wanted to make it my own. By adding layers of Apple Jalapeño Slaw, a decadent five-cheese bacon mac and another drizzle of the sweet and tangy BBQ sauce, the cone is elevated to epic proportions.

Serve these up at your next party and encourage your guests to pig out!

MAKES 12 SERVINGS

THE PIG-OUT CONE

Disposable aluminum half pan
Nonstick spray

5-CHEESE BACON MAC

1½ cups (173 g) shredded sharp cheddar cheese, divided

1½ cups (173 g) shredded Gouda cheese, divided

¾ cup (84 g) shredded Colby Jack cheese, divided

¾ cup (84 g) shredded Asiago cheese, divided

¾ cup (84 g) shredded Swiss cheese, divided

½ cup (30 g) panko bread crumbs

8 oz (225 g) thick-cut bacon, chopped, divided

5 tbsp (70 g) unsalted butter

6 tbsp (45 g) all-purpose flour

½ tsp kosher salt

¼ tsp freshly ground black pepper

¼ tsp dry mustard

¼ tsp onion powder

4 cups (946 ml) milk, whole

1 lb (455 g) medium-size shell macaroni, cooked al dente

TO ASSEMBLE

12 waffle cones

1 lb (455 g) leftover pulled pork (page 34), heated

Apple Jalapeño Slaw (page 22)

Memphis Mop BBQ Sauce (page 17), for brushing

Smoked maple syrup, for drizzling

(Continued)

Prepare a grill to cook (indirect) to medium-high heat, about 375°F (190°C). Set up the charcoal for 2-zone cooking. Light a charcoal chimney, and when the edges of the charcoal at the top of the chimney begin to ash over, dump the pile of hot coals onto 1 side of the grill to form your hot side (direct cooking), leaving the other side empty to form your cool side (indirect cooking), forming 2 zones.

Spray a disposable aluminum half pan with nonstick spray.

Prepare the 5-cheese bacon mac: In a medium-sized bowl, combine ½ cup (58 g) of the cheddar cheese, ½ cup (58 g) of the Gouda cheese, ¼ cup (28 g) of the Colby Jack cheese, ¼ cup (28 g) of the Asiago cheese, ¼ cup (28 g) of the Swiss cheese and the bread crumbs. Set this aside.

In a large, heavy-bottomed pot, cook the bacon over medium heat until it's browned and crisp. Transfer it to a paper towel–lined plate to drain any excess grease. Divide the bacon into 2 portions. Set aside 1 portion of the cooked bacon for the topping.

Remove all but 1 tablespoon (15 ml) of bacon grease from the pot and add the butter. Allow it to melt. Whisk in the flour and cook for 2 to 3 minutes. Add the salt, pepper, dry mustard and onion powder, stirring to combine them. Slowly pour in the milk, whisking constantly, while cooking until the mixture thickens, about 5 minutes.

Stir in the remaining cheeses and allow them to melt, adding 1 portion of the bacon and the cooked pasta. Pour the macaroni and cheese mixture into the prepared pan and top it with the cheese mixture and remaining portion of the bacon.

Place the pan on the grill over the indirect heat zone, close the lid and cook for 25 to 30 minutes, or until it's golden brown and bubbly.

Remove the pan from the cooker and let it rest for 5 to 10 minutes.

To assemble, layer each waffle cone with pulled pork, bacon mac, slaw, BBQ sauce and a drizzle of the smoked maple syrup.

NOTE: Smoked maple syrup is available at www.sugarbobsfinestkind.com.

A couple of years ago, I traveled with my family to Orange Beach, Alabama, to compete in the World Food Championships. During our stay in the Gulf Shores, our favorite place for breakfast was the Ruby Slipper Café. Known for adding a New Orleans flair to a hearty southern breakfast, the café offers an inspiring array of Benedicts on its menu. My version features a rich, golden BBQ hollandaise with a Memphis Mop BBQ Sauce base (page 17), which is tangy enough to stand up to smoked meats yet delicate enough to serve over eggs for breakfast or brunch. This recipe calls for pulled pork, but you can use smoked pork belly, bologna or even brisket.

MAKES 4 SERVINGS

Pork Benedict with BBQ Hollandaise

BBQ HOLLANDAISE

3 large egg yolks

2 tsp (10 ml) water

2 tbsp (30 ml) fresh lemon juice

2 tbsp (30 ml) Memphis Mop BBQ Sauce (page 17)

½ tsp dry mustard

½ tsp ancho chile powder

¼ tsp chipotle chile powder

½ cup (112 g) unsalted butter, melted

Kosher salt

Freshly ground black pepper

POACHED EGGS

2 cups (475 ml) water

2 tbsp (30 ml) distilled white vinegar

2 tsp (12 g) kosher salt

8 large eggs

4 slices Texas toast (see Note)

4 tbsp (55 g) unsalted butter, at room temperature

2 lbs (905 g) leftover pulled pork (page 34), heated

Chopped chives

Prepare the BBQ hollandaise: In a heatproof bowl or the top of a double boiler set over a pan of simmering water, vigorously whisk the egg yolks with the water until the mixture thickens, 3 to 4 minutes. Remove the bowl from the heat and stir in the lemon juice, BBQ sauce, dry mustard and ancho and chipotle powders.

Slowly whisk in the melted butter until the mixture thickens. Season with salt and black pepper to taste. Keep the sauce warm over gently simmering water, whisking occasionally, until ready to serve.

Poach the eggs: In a medium-sized saucepan, heat the water, vinegar and salt to a boil, then lower the heat to between 170 and 180°F (75 and 85°C). Working 1 at a time, crack an egg into a small bowl or cup. Stir the water in a clockwise direction to create a whirlpool. Once the water slows down slightly, place the bowl close to the surface of the hot water and gently slip the egg into the center of the whirlpool. Let the egg cook until the white fully sets and the yolk is no longer runny, about 3 minutes. Remove the egg with a slotted spoon and set it on a clean kitchen towel or a layer of paper towels to drain off as much liquid as possible. Repeat with the rest of the eggs.

While the eggs cook, toast the bread slices and coat one side of each slice with 1 tablespoon (14 g) of the butter, then set them aside.

To assemble the Benedicts, top each buttered toast slice with ½ cup (50 g) of the pulled pork, then 2 poached eggs. Spoon 1 tablespoon (15 ml) of the BBQ hollandaise over each egg and garnish with the chopped chives.

NOTE: Texas toast, despite its name, is not toasted prepackaging. It is a fresh loaf of bread that is sliced twice as thick as regular bread.

Sweet & Tangy
NORTH CAROLINA BBQ SAUCE

North Carolina's roots in southern barbecue run deep. In fact, battle lines have been drawn between variations in culinary styles. Not only are there different regions of barbecue within the state, there are opposing sauces, with each side claiming its sauce is the best.

Pork is the centerpiece of North Carolina BBQ. In the eastern part of the state, the meat is usually adorned with a peppery vinegar sauce. In the central and western parts of the state, tomato becomes a more prominent sauce component, mixed with vinegar and assorted spices.

I am not one who likes to choose sides, particularly when it comes to BBQ sauces. I love them all. When faced with the difficult decision of choosing just one, I tend to favor the sauce that is most versatile.

In this chapter, we will be preparing classics, such as Slow-Smoked Pork Shoulder (page 34) and Cheesy Smoked BBQ Meat Loaf (page 38). Then, we will be giving a southern twist to an old French favorite, chicken cordon bleu (page 37). Finally, we move on to creating what is quite possibly the ultimate hangover cure—the BBQ Bloody Mary (page 42)!

This sauce was inspired by my travels to North Carolina and the Tennessee Valley area as I was eating my way south. The sauce draws from the western Carolina tradition, so it has a vinegar base with a good amount of ketchup, rounded out with mustard and brown sugar. The finished sauce is a dark orange red and is not as thin as most Carolina sauces, making it a tangy and versatile accompaniment to pork, chicken and most other barbecue meats.

MAKES ABOUT 2½ CUPS (590 ML) SAUCE

North Carolina BBQ Sauce

1 cup (240 ml) cider vinegar

1 cup (240 ml) ketchup, such as Simply Heinz

⅓ cup (58 g) prepared yellow mustard

½ cup (115 g) packed light brown sugar

1 tsp Worcestershire sauce

1 tsp granulated garlic

1 tbsp (7 g) onion powder

1 tsp chili powder

¼ tsp cayenne pepper

1 tsp freshly ground black pepper

In a medium-sized saucepan, combine all the ingredients and bring it to a gentle boil over medium heat, stirring to dissolve the sugar. Lower the heat to low and simmer until it's slightly thickened, 20 to 25 minutes, stirring frequently. Let the sauce cool, transfer it to a jar and store it in the refrigerator for up to a month.

North Carolina BBQ sauce is the classic accompaniment to tender slow-smoked pork shoulder. Its sweet and tangy flavor profile complements the savory meat, whether you use it as a glaze to build a flavorful crust or mix it into the finished product to give it a bit more zing. This well-marbled piece of meat is loaded with flavorful fat and is ideal for smoking over low temperature.

MAKES 10 TO 12 SERVINGS

Slow-Smoked Pork Shoulder

1 (8- to 9-lbs [3.6- to 4-kg]) bone-in pork butt

¼ cup (44 g) prepared yellow mustard

1 cup (177 g) House Rub (page 71)

1 cup (240 ml) apple juice, plus more for spritzing

North Carolina BBQ Sauce (page 33), warmed, for brushing and serving

2 disposable aluminum half pans

Hickory or cherry wood

Trim the pork of any extra or loose-hanging fat. Leave the fat cap on, as this helps protect the butt and retain moisture during cooking. Pat the meat dry and rub all over with the mustard. Apply the house rub liberally to the meat. Place the butt in a disposable aluminum half pan. Cover the pan with plastic wrap and refrigerate it for at least an hour and up to 8 hours.

Prepare a smoker to cook at 250°F (120°C).

Once the cooker reaches temperature, add the wood, put the butt, fat side down, on the grate in the smoker and cook until the internal temperature reaches 160 to 170°F (71 to 77°C), about 6 hours, spritzing with apple juice every 30 minutes.

Remove the butt from the smoker. Pour 1 cup (240 ml) of the apple juice into a separate disposable aluminum pan and transfer the butt to the pan. Cover the pan with aluminum foil and place the pan in the smoker. Cook for another 2 to 3 hours, or until the internal temperature reaches 198 to 203°F (92 to 95°C).

Remove the pan from the smoker. Open the foil to vent for 10 minutes. Brush the BBQ sauce all over the butt. Return the butt to the pan and place it in the smoker for 20 minutes to set the sauce.

Remove the butt from the smoker and let rest, loosely covered with foil, for 30 minutes. Using heavy insulated gloves, gently pull the meat apart into large chunks. Discard the bone and any fat. Brush the chunks with a light coating of the BBQ sauce and set them aside. Shred or pull the remaining meat apart with your hands. Serve it with additional BBQ sauce on the side.

This is a grilled version of classic chicken cordon bleu. Rather than stuffing the chicken breasts and frying them, they are seasoned with dry rub and cooked directly over the coals before being glazed with the sweet and tangy BBQ sauce. The grilled breasts are then topped with slices of Virginia ham and an old southern favorite, pimiento cheese.

MAKES 4 SERVINGS

SOUTHERN CORDON BLEU

PIMIENTO CHEESE

8 oz (225 g) cream cheese, at room temperature

2 cups (240 g) grated extra-sharp cheddar cheese

½ cup (115 g) mayonnaise, such as Duke's

1½ tsp (7 ml) Worcestershire sauce

1½ tsp (4 g) dry mustard

1½ tsp (4 g) onion powder

1½ tsp (4 g) granulated garlic

¼ tsp paprika

½ cup (115 g) diced canned pimientos, drained

4 chicken breasts

Chicken Rub (page 112)

North Carolina BBQ Sauce (page 33), warmed, for brushing and dipping

8 slices Virginia ham

Prepare the pimiento cheese: In a food processor, pulse the cream cheese until whipped. Add the cheddar cheese, mayonnaise, Worcestershire, dry mustard, onion powder, granulated garlic and paprika and pulse to blend them. Add the diced pimientos and pulse a few times to combine them; refrigerate them for at least 1 hour, or until ready to use.

Set up a charcoal grill for 2-zone cooking. Light a charcoal chimney, and when the edges of the charcoal at the top of the chimney begin to ash over, dump the pile of hot coals onto 1 side of the grill to form your hot side (direct cooking), leaving the other side empty to form your cool side (indirect cooking), forming 2 zones.

Season the breasts with an even layer of the chicken rub to coat them. Place the chicken on the grate directly over the coals and cook until their internal temperature reaches 165°F (74°C), about 5 minutes per side. Brush the chicken with the warm BBQ sauce and move it to the indirect heat zone.

Grill the ham slices on the grate directly over the coals to warm them, 1 to 2 minutes per side.

To assemble the cordon bleu: Transfer the chicken to a sheet pan, place 2 slices of ham on each breast and top with ½ cup (65 g) of the pimiento cheese. Place the pan on the indirect heat side of the grill to slightly warm the cheese, 2 to 3 minutes. Remove the chicken from the cooker and let it rest for 5 minutes. Serve with a side of BBQ sauce for dipping.

When I think of comfort food my mind is immediately drawn to meat loaf. It is great as a main and even more delicious in sandwiches when left over. In this recipe, the BBQ sauce is mixed into the meat, then used as a glaze on top. The added kiss of smoke elevates this classic dish to a whole new level.

MAKES 4 TO 6 SERVINGS

Cheesy Smoked BBQ Meat Loaf

½ cup (120 ml) North Carolina BBQ Sauce (page 33), divided, plus ½ cup (120 ml) for serving

2 lbs (905 g) prime chuck

1 lb (455 g) pork sausage, such as Jimmy Dean

2 large eggs

1 cup (115 g) dried bread crumbs

2 cups (225 g) shredded cheddar cheese

1 tbsp (9 g) granulated garlic

1 tsp onion powder

1 tsp salt

1 tsp freshly ground black pepper

Nonstick spray

House Rub (page 71)

2 (9 x 5" [23 x 12.5–cm]) aluminum foil loaf pans

Hickory wood

Prepare the meat loaf: In a large bowl, using ¼ cup (60 ml) of the BBQ sauce and reserving the rest, mix together the prime chuck, sausage, eggs, bread crumbs, cheese, garlic, onion powder, salt and pepper until they're just combined, being careful not to overmix the meat.

Prepare the two loaf pans by lining each pan with a piece of plastic wrap that is twice the size of the pan, leaving the excess wrap hanging over the sides.

Cut the meat loaf mixture in half and gently press each half down into a prepared loaf pan. Cover the pans with the overhanging plastic wrap and refrigerate them for 1 hour.

Prepare a smoker to cook at 275°F (140°C). Line a sheet pan with aluminum foil, spray a baking rack with nonstick spray and place the rack on top of the foil.

Once the cooker reaches temperature, add the wood and unmold the meat loaves onto the rack-topped sheet pan.

Lightly dust the loaves with house rub and place the sheet pan in the smoker. Cook for about 1 hour 45 minutes, or until the loaves reach an internal temperature of 150°F (66°C), starting to check the temperature at the 90-minute mark.

Glaze the meat with the reserved North Carolina BBQ sauce and return the pan to the cooker until the loaves reach an internal temperature of 160°F (71°C), about 15 minutes.

Remove the meat loaves from the smoker and let them rest for 10 minutes. Slice and serve them with the remaining BBQ sauce on the side for dipping.

Pulled chicken is a great alternative to pulled pork when you need something quick and easy but don't want to compromise on flavor. You can pull or shred the leftover chicken and blend it with the North Carolina BBQ Sauce (page 33) before placing it on the bun. Top it with the Carolina slaw for an extra kick and added crunch.

MAKES 4 SERVINGS

Pulled Chicken Sandwich with Carolina Slaw

CAROLINA SLAW

⅓ cup (80 ml) olive oil

2 tbsp (30 ml) cider vinegar

2 tbsp (26 g) sugar

1 tsp salt

¼ tsp freshly ground black pepper

½ tsp celery seeds

1 (1-lb [455-g]) package coleslaw mix

1 small onion, sliced thinly

2 Smoked Chicken Halves (page 156), heated

½ cup (120 ml) North Carolina BBQ Sauce (page 33), warmed, plus more for drizzling

4 brioche buns

Prepare the slaw: In a medium-sized bowl, whisk together the olive oil, vinegar, sugar, salt, pepper and celery seeds. Add the coleslaw mix and onion and toss to coat them. Cover the bowl and refrigerate it until ready to use.

Pull the chicken: Remove all the meat from the chicken and shred it. Discard the skin. Add the chicken to the warm BBQ sauce and mix well.

Pile the pulled chicken on the lower halves of the buns and drizzle with extra BBQ sauce. Top them with the Carolina slaw and close the sandwiches to serve.

More than a few people have told me that my North Carolina BBQ Sauce (page 33) was so good that they could drink it! Here's your chance to see what all the fuss is about. If you are a fan of Bloody Marys, this recipe is sure to spice up your brunch or even a morning tailgate. It's sweet and smoky with just the right amount of heat and is sure to cure what ails ya. Don't be afraid to get creative and garnish it with all your barbecue favorites.

MAKES ABOUT 8 SERVINGS

BBQ Bloody Mary

8 cups (1.9 L) tomato juice

1 cup (240 ml) vodka, or to taste

⅓ cup (80 ml) North Carolina BBQ Sauce (page 33), or to taste

⅓ cup (80 ml) fresh lemon juice

3 tbsp (45 ml) Worcestershire sauce

2 to 3 tsp (10 to 15 ml) hot sauce, such as Crystal

1 tsp celery salt

1 tbsp (15 g) prepared horseradish

Salt and freshly ground black pepper

Lime or lemon wedges, for rim

House Rub (page 71)

SUGGESTED GARNISHES

Lime wedges

Lemon wedges

Celery ribs

Grilled shrimp

Cooked bacon

Olives

In a large pitcher, stir together the tomato juice, vodka, BBQ sauce, lemon juice, Worcestershire, hot sauce, celery salt, horseradish and salt and pepper to taste.

Moisten the rim of each glass with a lime or lemon wedge, then dip the rims in the house rub. Fill the glasses with ice and the tomato juice mixture. Garnish the drinks with lime and lemon wedges, celery, grilled shrimp, bacon or olives, if desired.

Honey
BBQ SAUCE

When springtime approaches, I find myself daydreaming of the summer's bounty that will soon be available at my local farmers' market. In recent years, these markets have grown increasingly popular and their selections have broadened as a result. While the focus remains on fresh produce, it is not uncommon to find free-range chicken, uncured pork belly and other locally sourced items, including BBQ sauces, rubs and honey.

Unscrewing the cap on the first jar of local honey I ever purchased revealed a golden treasure. Vastly different than the mass-produced grocery store variety, it had a beautiful amber hue, a penetrating honey flavor with a mild finish and just the right amount of sweetness. Instinctively, my mind, and my taste buds, told me this would make a great honey-infused BBQ sauce!

The recipes in this chapter focus on grilled or smoked tailgate favorites, with ingredients that are readily available in most farmers' markets.

Rich colors of amber and brown form the tapestry that makes up this sticky, sweet honey sauce. The vinegar and mustard in this recipe provide a mild kick that gets rounded out by the sauce's buttery finish. This sauce goes great with chicken, beef or pork and will elevate your barbecue to such new heights that you might even be inclined to eat it right out of the jar!

MAKES ABOUT 3 CUPS (710 ML) SAUCE

Honey BBQ Sauce

1 cup (240 ml) ketchup, such as Simply Heinz

1 cup (240 ml) distilled white vinegar

2 tbsp (40 g) molasses

1 cup (340 g) honey

1 tsp salt

½ tsp freshly ground black pepper

2 tbsp (22 g) prepared yellow mustard

1 tsp paprika

1½ tsp (4 g) granulated garlic

1½ tsp (4 g) onion powder

In a medium-sized saucepan, combine all the ingredients and bring it to a gentle boil over medium heat, stirring frequently. Lower the heat to low and simmer until the sauce is slightly thickened, 10 to 15 minutes, stirring frequently. Remove the pan from the heat, let it cool, transfer the sauce to a jar and store it in the refrigerator for up to a month.

Beer can chicken is one of those essential recipes that all cooks should have in their back pocket. Also referred to as "chicken on a throne," it is a barbecued chicken dish whose method of indirect grilling uses a partially filled can of beer that is placed in the chicken's cavity prior to cooking. The steam from the evaporating beer helps keep the inside of the bird moist, while the outside develops a crisp skin that is then glazed with the sticky, sweet BBQ sauce.

MAKES 4 SERVINGS

Beer Can Chicken

1 tbsp (19 g) kosher salt

1 tbsp (6 g) freshly ground black pepper

1 tbsp (9 g) granulated garlic

1 tbsp (7 g) paprika

1 tbsp (4 g) ground thyme

1 (4- to 5-lb [1.8- to 2.3-kg]) chicken

2 tbsp (30 ml) olive oil

1 (12-oz [355-ml]) can of your favorite beer

1 to 2 sprigs rosemary

2 cloves garlic, crushed with the back of a knife

Honey BBQ Sauce (page 47), warmed, for brushing and dipping

Set up a charcoal grill for 2-zone cooking around 350°F (180°C). Light a charcoal chimney, and when the edges of the charcoal at the top of the chimney begin to ash over, dump the pile of hot coals onto 1 side of the grill to form your hot side (direct cooking), leaving the other side empty to form your cool side (indirect cooking), forming 2 zones.

In a small bowl, combine the salt, pepper, granulated garlic, paprika and thyme. Rub the chicken all over with the olive oil, then season the bird with the spice mixture.

Open the beer and drink about one-third of it because, why not? It is your favorite! Add the rosemary and crushed garlic to the can and gently swish the can around to mix them.

Lower the chicken onto the open can so that the chicken is sitting upright with the can in its cavity, legs out front, kind of like a tripod.

Once the grill reaches temperature, place the chicken on the grill over the indirect heat zone and close the lid. Cook until the chicken reaches an internal temperature of 180°F (82°C) in the thickest part of the thigh and 165°F (74°C) in the breast, about 1½ hours.

Brush the chicken with the warm BBQ sauce and close the lid. Continue to cook for 12 to 15 minutes to set the glaze. Remove the chicken from the grill and allow it to rest for 15 minutes before carving. Serve with a side of BBQ sauce for dipping.

Atomic buffalo turds, aka ABTs, are essentially slow-smoked jalapeño poppers that are stuffed with cream cheese and a variety of fillings before being wrapped in bacon, smoked and glazed with BBQ sauce. Although this recipe has evolved over time with a few additions, it has remained quite the crowd-pleaser. In fact, once I added this savory honey BBQ sauce as a glaze for these ABTs, I won my first bacon cook-off!

MAKES 20 SERVINGS

ABTs: Atomic Buffalo Turds Stuffed with Sausage & Cheese

1 cup (230 g) cream cheese, at room temperature

1 cup (115 g) shredded sharp cheddar cheese

2 tsp (7 g) House Rub (page 71), plus more for seasoning

10 jalapeño peppers, cut in half lengthwise and seeded

10 Lit'l Smokies or andouille sausages, cut in half lengthwise

10 slices bacon, cut in half crosswise

Honey BBQ Sauce (page 47), warmed, for brushing

Wooden toothpicks, for securing bacon (optional)

Hickory or pecan wood

If using, soak the toothpicks in a shallow bowl of water for 1 hour before cooking.

Prepare a smoker to cook at 275°F (140°C). Line a sheet pan with aluminum foil.

In a medium-sized bowl, mix together the cream cheese, cheddar cheese and 2 teaspoons (7 g) of house rub. Fill the hollowed-out portion of the peppers with the cheese mixture.

Place a sausage on top of each cream cheese–stuffed pepper and wrap it with ½ a slice of bacon so that the seam is on the bottom. Secure it with a toothpick, if necessary. Dust the peppers all over with more house rub and arrange them on the prepared sheet pan.

Once the cooker reaches temperature, add the wood and place the pan in the smoker.

Cook until the bacon is crisp and the peppers are tender, 1 to 1½ hours. Brush them with the BBQ sauce and continue to cook for 5 to 10 minutes to set the glaze. Remove the poppers from the cooker and let them rest for 10 minutes, as the filling will be hot. Arrange the poppers on a platter to serve.

Who doesn't love appetizers, especially ones that are almost healthy for you? These bacon-wrapped Brussels sprouts are a great way to increase the vegetables in your diet, as well as the bacon! As the Brussels sprouts become tender and the bacon crisp, brush them with the BBQ sauce for an insanely addictive bite. You'll love the way the sweetness of the sauce balances the bitterness of the Brussels sprouts. Serve this sweet and smoky finger food at your next tailgate or holiday party.

MAKES ABOUT 8 SERVINGS

Bacon-Wrapped Smoked Brussels Sprouts

Nonstick spray

1 lb (455 g) Brussels sprouts, ends trimmed and discolored leaves removed

8 oz (225 g) thick-sliced bacon, cut in half crosswise

3 tbsp (33 g) House Rub (page 71)

Honey BBQ Sauce (page 47), warmed, for brushing and dipping

Wooden toothpicks, for securing bacon

Hickory wood

Soak the toothpicks in a shallow bowl of water for 1 hour before cooking.

Prepare a smoker to cook at 300°F (150°C). Line a sheet pan with aluminum foil. Spray a baking rack with nonstick spray and place it on top of the foil.

Wrap each Brussels sprout in ½ slice of bacon and secure it with a toothpick. Dust each sprout with the house rub, covering all sides. Place them on the rack-topped sheet pan.

Once the smoker reaches temperature, add the wood and place the pan in the cooker. Cook for about 1 hour, then brush the sprouts with the BBQ sauce and return the pan to the smoker. Cook until the bacon crisps up and the sprouts become tender, about 15 minutes.

Serve with BBQ sauce on the side for dipping.

My favorite dish at Hubba Hubba Smokehouse in Flat Rock, North Carolina, is the loaded sweet potato stuffed with pulled pork. The creamy potato, topped with all the fixings, was a nice contrast to the smoky pork. The addition of the smoked candied pecans and the sweet and tangy honey BBQ sauce really puts this dish over the top! Here's my version.

MAKES ABOUT 4 SERVINGS

Loaded BBQ Sweet Potato with Pulled Pork & Smoked Candied Pecans

SMOKED CANDIED PECANS
Nonstick spray
12 oz (340 g) pecan halves
½ cup (120 ml) melted butter
1 tbsp (11 g) House Rub (page 71)
½ cup (120 ml) pure maple syrup

4 medium-sized sweet potatoes or yams
Olive oil
Kosher salt
1 lb (455 g) leftover pulled pork (page 34), heated
½ cup (120 ml) Honey BBQ Sauce (page 47), warmed, plus more for drizzling
4 tbsp (56 g) unsalted butter
1 cup (115 g) shredded sharp cheddar cheese
½ cup (40 g) cooked and crumbled bacon
½ cup (50 g) thinly sliced scallion
Sour cream
Apple or pecan wood

Prepare a smoker to cook at 275°F (140°C). Line a sheet pan with aluminum foil and spray with nonstick spray.

Prepare the pecans: In a medium-sized bowl, combine the pecans, melted butter, house rub and maple syrup. Spread the pecans in a single layer on the prepared pan. Once the cooker reaches temperature, add the wood and place the pan in the smoker to cook for 25 to 30 minutes. Remove the pan of pecans from the cooker and set it aside to cool.

Kick up the temperature in your smoker to 300°F (150°C).

Scrub the sweet potatoes under cool water to remove any dirt and dry them with paper towels. Brush them with olive oil and sprinkle on salt. Once the cooker reaches temperature, place the potatoes directly on the grate in the smoker and cook until they're tender, 1½ to 1¾ hours. Add the pork to the warm BBQ sauce and mix well.

Cut a slit lengthwise in each potato and fluff the insides with a fork. Stuff them with the butter, pork, cheddar cheese, bacon, scallion and sour cream to your liking. Arrange the sweet potatoes on a platter and top with the candied pecans and a drizzle of the BBQ sauce to serve.

Smoking these thick-cut bacon skewers is like having candied bacon crack on a stick. This meat candy isn't for the faint of heart. The honey BBQ sauce helps create a sweet, salty, sticky and smoky bite that is so very satisfying.

MAKES ABOUT 16 SERVINGS

Thick-Cut Bacon Skewers

1 cup (225 g) packed light brown sugar

1 lb (455 g) thick-cut bacon

House Rub (page 71)

Honey BBQ Sauce (page 47), warmed, for brushing and dipping

Wooden skewers, soaked in water for at least 20 minutes

Hickory wood or cherry wood

Prepare a smoker to cook at 325°F (170°C). Alternatively, you can prepare this recipe on your grill over indirect heat, utilizing the two-zone cooking method. Be sure to place a drip pan underneath to avoid flare-ups. Set up a charcoal grill for 2-zone cooking. Light a charcoal chimney, and when the edges of the charcoal at the top of the chimney begin to ash over, dump the pile of hot coals onto 1 side of the grill to form your hot side (direct cooking), leaving the other side empty to form your cool side (indirect cooking), forming 2 zones. Line 2 sheet pans with aluminum foil. Fit an additional sheet pan with a baking rack, to use for cooling.

Place the brown sugar in a 1-gallon (4-L) ziplock bag. Toss in the bacon slices, 1 at a time, to coat them, then dust each side of the bacon with the house rub. To thread the bacon onto the soaked skewers, fold each slice accordion style and push the skewer through the center or meat section of each slice, rather than through the fat. Once on the skewer, fan out the bacon a bit. Place the skewers on the foil-lined sheet pans.

Once the smoker reaches temperature, add the wood and place the sheet pans on the grate to cook for 15 minutes. (If using a charcoal grill, place the bacon skewers directly on the grate, over the indirect heat side of the grill, and cook with the lid closed for 15 minutes.) Then, carefully flip each bacon skewer over and return to the smoker/grill. Cook for another 10 minutes and brush them with the BBQ sauce. Cook until the bacon is just done and the sauce is set, 5 to 10 minutes more, keeping an eye on the skewers to prevent them from overcooking. Remove the pan from the cooker and immediately transfer the bacon skewers to the rack-topped sheet pan to cool. Make sure the bacon skewers do not touch while cooling, as they could stick together. Allow them to cool for 5 minutes, then arrange them on a platter to serve with BBQ sauce on the side for dipping.

Sweet & Smoky
KANSAS CITY BBQ SAUCE

Kansas City barbecue is a melting pot of flavors and styles from all over the country, resulting in an award-winning cuisine that is synonymous with the American barbecue tradition. It is characterized by its use of a wide variety of meats, serving up everything from pork, beef and chicken to turkey, lamb and sausage, slow-smoked over a wood fire and slathered in sauce. Kansas City BBQ sauce is a sweet and thick tomato-based sauce that's often mixed with brown sugar, molasses and varying combinations of spices.

Every year, people from all over the world make the pilgrimage to Kansas City, just to get a sample of the city's acclaimed cuisine. This cuisine is so endeared that the mission of the Kansas City Barbeque Society, a nonprofit organization, is to celebrate, teach, preserve and promote barbecue as a culinary technique, sport and art form.

In this chapter, I will show you how to infuse some of that Kansas City BBQ love into the menu at your next cookout. Recipes will cover smoking a fatty (page 72), making Moink Balls (page 71), the best, most luscious bite in the biz (Brisket Burnt Ends [page 62]), a smoked tri-tip cheese steak sandwich (page 65) and the ultimate Smoked Surf & Turf BBQ Burger with BBQ Aioli (page 68). Now we're beginning to understand why Kansas City BBQ is loved by so many people, right?

Kansas City sauce is arguably the most popular sauce style in American barbecue, and it is likely the first thing that comes to mind when many people think of barbecue. I am proud to say that this sauce has helped me win many top 10 awards at BBQ contests without the addition of any artificial flavor enhancers, plus it's my son's favorite sauce. My version of this classic, dark sauce is not quite as thick as most other Kansas City variants, and the pineapple juice helps provide a bright finish to its sweet, smoky flavors.

MAKES ABOUT 2½ CUPS (590 ML) SAUCE

Kansas City BBQ Sauce

1¼ cups (295 ml) ketchup, such as Simply Heinz

1 cup (225 g) packed light brown sugar

¼ cup (85 g) molasses

¼ cup (60 ml) pineapple juice

¼ cup (60 ml) water

1 tbsp (15 ml) natural hickory liquid smoke

2½ tsp (8 g) dry mustard

2 tsp (5 g) smoked paprika

½ tsp granulated garlic

1½ tsp (9 g) kosher salt

1 tsp freshly ground black pepper

Pinch of cayenne pepper

In a medium-sized saucepan combine all the ingredients and bring it to a gentle boil over medium heat, stirring to dissolve the sugar. Reduce the heat to low and simmer until slightly thickened, 20 to 25 minutes, stirring occasionally. Let the sauce cool, transfer it to a jar and store it in the refrigerator for up to a month.

In Kansas City, barbecued burnt ends are considered a delicacy. Great care is taken in producing these smoky, melt in your mouth bites of rich, fatty beef. Once cooked, the burnt ends are cut into cubes from the "point," or fat end, of the brisket. Then they are seasoned again, glazed with the sweet BBQ sauce and cooked further to fully render the fat, resulting in the ultimate barbecue bite.

MAKES 6 TO 8 SERVINGS

Brisket Burnt Ends

1 (6- to 9-lb [2.7- to 4.1-kg]) choice-grade brisket point

Olive oil

1 tbsp (19 g) kosher salt

1 tbsp (6 g) freshly ground black pepper

1 tbsp (9 g) granulated garlic

½ cup (120 ml) beef broth

1 cup (240 ml) Kansas City BBQ Sauce (page 61)

3 large, disposable aluminum pans

Hickory, oak or pecan wood

Place the brisket point in a large, disposable aluminum pan and rub it all over with the olive oil.

In a small bowl, mix together the salt, pepper and granulated garlic. Sprinkle the spice mixture evenly over the meat and press firmly with your hand to adhere the spice.

Cover the pan and refrigerate it for at least 4 hours and up to overnight.

One hour before you plan to cook, take the brisket out and allow it to come to room temperature.

Prepare the smoker to cook at 275°F (140°C).

Once the cooker reaches temperature, add the wood and place the pan in the smoker. Cook until the brisket reaches an internal temperature of 165°F (74°C), 4 to 5 hours.

Transfer the brisket to a separate large, disposable aluminum pan and pour the beef broth around the meat. Cover the pan with aluminum foil and place it in the smoker. Cook until the brisket reaches an internal temperature of 198 to 203°F (92 to 95°C) and a thermometer pushed into the meat gives little resistance, 2 to 3 hours.

(Continued)

Brisket Burnt Ends (Continued)

Remove the pan from the smoker and open the foil to vent for 10 to 15 minutes. Strain the accumulated juices of their fat and set that aside. Transfer the brisket to a cutting board and cut it into 1-inch (2.5-cm) cubes. Place the meat in a fresh disposable aluminum pan, add ¼ cup (60 ml) of the reserved liquid and the BBQ sauce and place it back on the cooker for 1 hour. Remove the pan from the smoker and gently coat the burnt ends with the sauce, then place it back on the cooker for 15 minutes to set the glaze. Arrange the burnt ends on a platter to serve.

NOTE: This recipe can also be made by reserving the cooked brisket point from the Texas-Style Beef Brisket (page 80). It is easy to do once the brisket is cooked and rested. Simply transfer the meat to a large cutting board and, using a long carving knife, follow along the line of fat between the muscles and separate the flat from the point. Cut the point meat into 1-inch (2.5-cm) cubes. Place the meat in a disposable aluminum pan, add ¼ cup (60 ml) of beef broth and 1 cup (240 ml) of the BBQ sauce and place the pan back on the cooker for 1 hour. Remove it from the smoker and gently coat the burnt ends with the sauce, then place the pan back on the cooker for 15 minutes to set the glaze. Arrange the meat on a platter to serve.

This barbecue-inspired steak sandwich is my take on the Philly classic. It has many of the same components as the original sandwich, such as onions, beef and cheese, but it gets its boost of flavor from caramelized onions that are simmered in a sweet and smoky BBQ sauce and beer mixture. Be sure to serve these "cheesesteaks" on a crusty roll to catch all the juicy, saucy drippings.

NOTE: Tri tip steak is one of the most versatile and flavorful cuts of meat that can be smoked in under two hours. Cut from the bottom sirloin of a steer, it is a large, tender, triangular muscle, AKA as the Santa Maria steak.

MAKES 4 SERVINGS

Smoked "Philly-Style" Tri Tip Steak Sandwich with Provolone, Peppers & BBQ Onions

1 (2½-lb [1.1-kg]) tri tip steak
Salt and freshly ground black pepper
2 differently colored bell peppers, seeded and quartered
2 tbsp (30 ml) olive oil

BBQ ONIONS

1 tbsp (15 ml) olive oil
4 large onions, sliced
1 tbsp (11 g) House Rub (page 71)
2 cloves garlic, minced
½ cup (120 ml) Kansas City BBQ Sauce (page 61), plus more for drizzling
½ cup (120 ml) beer
1 tbsp (11 g) Dijon mustard
1 tbsp (15 ml) balsamic vinegar
2 tsp (10 ml) soy sauce

TO ASSEMBLE

4 hoagie/sub rolls, such as Amoroso
8 slices provolone cheese

Oak or hickory wood

(Continued)

Smoked "Philly-Style" Tri Tip Steak Sandwich with Provolone, Peppers and BBQ Onions (Continued)

Prepare a smoker to cook at 250°F (120°C). Line a sheet pan with aluminum foil.

Season the tri tip all over with the salt and pepper and let it sit out for about an hour.

Brush each bell pepper quarter with olive oil and season with salt and black pepper. Arrange the bell peppers on the prepared sheet pan and set them aside until you are ready to cook.

Once the cooker reaches temperature, add the wood and place the pan of peppers on a rack in your cooker. Place the tri tip directly on the grate of another rack in the smoker and cook both the peppers and steak for 1 to 1½ hours, or until the peppers are tender and the steak reaches an internal temperature of 130 to 135°F (54 to 57°C) for medium rare. Remove the steak from the cooker and wrap it in foil. Allow the meat to rest for about 20 minutes.

Allow the peppers to cool, then cut them into ¼-inch (6-mm) slices.

Prepare the onions: In a large sauté pan, heat the olive oil over medium heat. Add the onions and cook, stirring occasionally, until they're tender and just beginning to brown, 20 to 25 minutes. Add the house rub and garlic. Cook for 2 to 3 minutes and then stir in the BBQ sauce, beer, Dijon, vinegar and soy sauce. Simmer, uncovered, stirring occasionally, until the mixture thickens slightly, about 10 minutes.

Assemble the sandwiches: Slice open the rolls and warm them on a sheet pan in the smoker for 5 minutes. Remove the rolls from the cooker and layer each with 2 slices of cheese. Slice the meat against the grain into thin strips, layering it onto the rolls along with the onions and peppers. Drizzle the sandwiches with BBQ sauce to serve.

On my quest to create the ultimate surf-and-turf burger, I found that the smoke elevates the flavor of the meat, while the BBQ aioli ties it all together with the bacon-wrapped shrimp. The burger blend that I created was designed to remain tender, moist and flavorful throughout the long cook.

MAKES 6 SERVINGS

Smoked Surf & Turf BBQ Burger with BBQ Aioli

BBQ AIOLI

1 large egg yolk

¼ cup (60 ml) vegetable oil

1 tbsp (15 ml) Kansas City BBQ Sauce (page 61), plus more for drizzling

Salt

1 tsp fresh lemon juice, or to taste

BURGERS

2¼ lbs (1 kg) burger blend (chuck, prime short rib, bacon) or 80/20 ground beef

Worcestershire sauce

Salt and freshly ground black pepper

6 slices cheddar cheese (optional)

TO ASSEMBLE

6 tbsp (84 g) unsalted butter

6 hamburger buns

6 thick slices tomato

6 green leaf lettuce leaves

6 Crab-Stuffed Bacon-Wrapped Shrimp, tail off (page 132), heated

Hickory wood

Prepare a smoker to cook at 275°F (140°C). Fit a sheet pan with a baking rack.

Prepare the BBQ aioli: In a small bowl, whisk the egg yolk for 30 seconds. Slowly add the oil, drop by drop, until an emulsion forms, and then whisk in the rest in a slow stream until all the oil is incorporated. Whisk in the BBQ sauce and season with salt and lemon juice to taste. Cover and refrigerate the aioli until ready to use.

Prepare the burgers: Using your hands, form the meat into 6 burger patties. Brush the patties with a light coating of Worcestershire and season them with salt and pepper to your liking. Using your thumb, press a small indentation into the bottom of each burger to keep it from bulging up as it cooks. Place the burgers on a rack-topped sheet pan.

Once the cooker reaches temperature, add the wood and place the pan on the grate in the smoker. Cook for about 45 minutes, then place the cheddar cheese on the burgers (if using). Check the temperature of the burgers at the 1-hour mark and cook until they reach an internal temperature of 160°F (71°C).

Assemble the burgers: Butter the interior side of each bun with 1 tablespoon (14 g) of the butter and grill or toast the buttered side until it's crispy. Spread 1 tablespoon (15 ml) of the BBQ aioli on the bottom bun, then layer with a burger, a tomato slice, a lettuce leaf and a bacon-wrapped shrimp. Top it all off with a drizzle of BBQ sauce and a bun top to serve.

These bacon-wrapped meatballs are a highly addictive appetizer that gets its name from beef (moo) and pork (oink). They are rubbed, grilled and then glazed to perfection.

MAKES ABOUT 24 SERVINGS

MOINK BALLS

HOUSE RUB

1 cup (200 g) raw cane sugar

⅔ cup (80 g) chili powder

½ cup (144 g) sea salt

¼ cup (28 g) onion powder

¼ cup (36 g) granulated garlic

¼ cup (28 g) paprika

1 tbsp (7 g) ground cumin

2 tsp (4 g) cayenne pepper

1 tsp ground thyme

1½ lbs (680 g) ground beef, 80/20

¾ cup (90 g) seasoned dried bread crumbs

⅓ cup (33 g) grated Parmesan cheese

2 large eggs

1 tbsp (4 g) chopped fresh parsley

2 cloves garlic, minced

2 tsp (4 g) Italian seasoning

1 lb (455 g) bacon, cut in half widthwise

¾ cup (175 ml) Kansas City BBQ Sauce (page 61)

Wooden toothpicks, for securing bacon

Hickory wood or cherry wood

Soak the toothpicks in a shallow bowl of water for 1 hour before cooking.

Prepare the rub: In a medium-sized bowl, combine all the rub ingredients and set it aside. Leftover rub may be stored in an airtight container for up to 6 months.

Prepare a smoker or charcoal grill to cook at 375°F (190°C). If using, set up the charcoal grill for 2-zone cooking. Light a charcoal chimney, and when the edges of the charcoal at the top of the chimney begin to ash over, dump the pile of hot coals onto 1 side of the grill to form your hot side (direct cooking), leaving the other side empty to form your cool side (indirect cooking), forming 2 zones.

In a large bowl, combine the ground beef, bread crumbs, Parmesan cheese, eggs, parsley, garlic and Italian seasoning and mix thoroughly.

Form the meat into 1-ounce (28-g) balls. Wrap each meatball with a ½ slice of bacon and secure it with a toothpick. Sprinkle the meatballs evenly with ¼ cup (44 g) of the house rub.

If using a smoker, once the cooker reaches temperature, add the wood and place the meatballs, seam side down, directly on the cooking grate. If grilling, place the meatballs on the indirect heat side with the grill lid on.

After about 20 minutes, glaze the meatballs with the BBQ sauce and place them back on the cooker for another 10 minutes, or until the meatballs reach an internal temperature of 160°F (71°C). Let them rest for 5 minutes. Serve as a snack or appetizer.

When I first got into barbecue, I had heard the folklore of the barbecued fatty, aka the bacon explosion. I couldn't believe there was such a thing as breakfast sausage stuffed with varying combinations of eggs, cheese, hash browns, diced ham, peppers, onions and you name it. Then, the whole thing is wrapped in bacon, seasoned with rub, smoked and glazed with this sweet and smoky BBQ sauce! Wow! It's for real and it's amazing. For an extra-special treat, serve each slice with a drizzle of maple syrup.

MAKES 6 TO 8 SERVINGS

Breakfast Fatty

12 strips bacon

1 lb (455 g) breakfast sausage meat

Nonstick spray

¾ cup (170 g) cooked hash browns

3 large eggs, scrambled

½ cup (58 g) shredded cheddar cheese

2 tbsp (20 g) diced onion, sautéed

2 tbsp (19 g) seeded and diced green bell pepper, sautéed

House Rub (page 71)

Kansas City BBQ Sauce (page 61), warmed, for brushing and dipping

Hickory wood

Prepare the bacon weave: Lay out 6 strips of the bacon closely in parallel on a piece of parchment paper. Alternating strips, fold back the ends of 3 of them just enough to accommodate a seventh slice of bacon being laid perpendicular across the 3 nonfolded strips, then unfold the 3 folded strips to lie flat across the added slice. Next, fold back the *other* 3 strips in the *other* direction, adding another (the eighth) slice of bacon perpendicular to the first added slice and then unfolding the 3 folded strips to lie across that. Repeat, adding 1 slice at a time of the 4 remaining slices of bacon, alternating which 3 strips are folded back as you do so, to complete the weave. Place in the refrigerator until ready to use.

Prepare a smoker to cook at 275°F (140°C).

Place the breakfast sausage meat in a gallon-sized (4-L) ziplock bag and flatten out the meat until it reaches an even thickness. Use scissors to cut away the plastic bag and transfer the sausage patty to a piece of aluminum foil that has been sprayed with nonstick spray. Top it with the hash browns, scrambled eggs, cheddar cheese, onion and bell pepper.

(Continued)

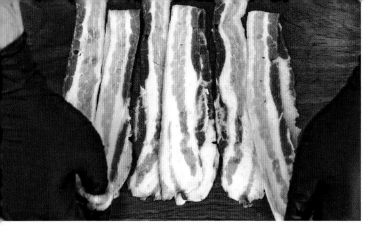

Fold back even numbered strips

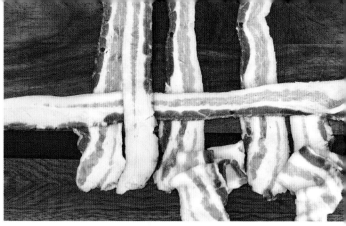

Lay a slice of bacon perpendicular to the folded bacon

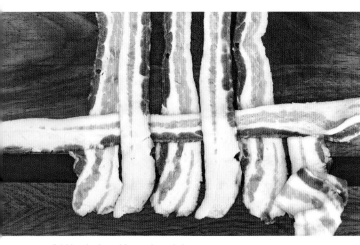

Now fold back the odd numbered slices

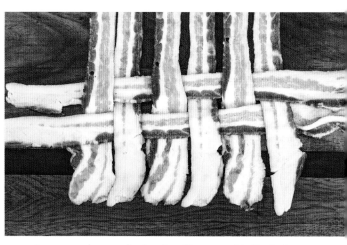

Lay a second perpendicular slice of bacon next to the first, then unfold the odd numbered strips over it

Repeat until all of the bacon is used

The smoked fatty

Breakfast Fatty (Continued)

Roll up the sausage into a log shape and place it along one edge of the bacon weave. Tightly roll up the sausage in the bacon weave and season it with the house rub.

Once the cooker reaches temperature, add the wood and place the fatty on the grate in the smoker. Cook for about 1½ hours, or until the fatty reaches an internal temperature of 165°F (74°C). Brush it with the warm BBQ sauce and continue to cook for 10 minutes to set the glaze. Transfer the fatty to a platter and tent it loosely with foil. Allow it to rest for about 25 minutes. Slice and serve the fatty with BBQ sauce on the side for dipping.

Bold Texas
BBQ SAUCE

Barbecue in the Lone Star state draws on the many diverse cultural traditions of its people, creating several distinct styles. In east Texas, we find barbecue traditions closer to those of the Deep South, where beef, as well as pork, are served with spicy BBQ sauce. The state's historical connections with Mexican cuisine may explain the influence of certain ingredients, including chile pepper, tomato and cayenne.

The flavors of Texas barbecue are bold yet simple. Spice rubs rely heavily on salt and pepper, allowing the flavor of the meat to shine. The use of highly seasoned sauce is rather subtle and complements the smoky meats. Whereas some pitmasters use the sauce to help form a flavorful crust during the long, slow-cooking process, others serve it alongside the finished product.

In this chapter you will get the recipe for my Award-Winning "Triple B" Smoked Chili (page 89), make pulled BBQ Beef Tacos (page 83), learn the secrets to making tender Sweet & Spicy Beef Back Ribs (page 86) and use leftover brisket to make one of my favorite side dishes—a hearty pot of sweet and spicy Brisket Baked Beans (page 90). This is the kind of food that brings people together in celebration of outdoor cooking. It is meant to be shared among family, friends and neighbors.

In some parts of Texas, they ridicule the use of BBQ sauce, yet in other parts you'll find a tomato-based sauce with a hint of zing. My version is a spicy and tangy sauce that draws bold flavor from chili powder, pepper, garlic, vinegar and Worcestershire sauce, balanced against a subtle sweetness. The finished sauce has a deep reddish-brown color, and is somewhat thinner in texture, which makes it great for mopping meats during cooking, yet versatile enough to use as a finishing sauce.

MAKES ABOUT 2 CUPS (475 ML) SAUCE

Texas BBQ Sauce

1½ cups (355 ml) ketchup, such as Simply Heinz

3 tbsp (45 ml) cider vinegar

2 tbsp (30 ml) Worcestershire sauce

¼ cup (60 g) packed light brown sugar

1 tsp smoked paprika

1 tsp granulated garlic

1 tsp chili powder

2 tsp (5 g) onion powder

¼ to ½ tsp cayenne pepper (depending on how much of a kick you prefer)

3 tbsp (60 g) molasses

2 tsp (8 g) prepared yellow mustard

In a medium-sized saucepan, combine all the ingredients and bring it to a gentle boil over medium heat, stirring to dissolve the sugar. Lower the heat to low and simmer until it's slightly thickened, 15 to 20 minutes, stirring frequently. Let the sauce cool, transfer it to a jar and store it in the refrigerator for up to a month.

In Texas barbecue, a smoky, peppery and tender brisket is king. A whole packer brisket is generously seasoned with just salt and pepper (aka Dalmatian rub), then slow-smoked for hours over the low heat of a wood or charcoal fire. I like to serve its bold sauce on the side as it is the perfect complement to the smoky meat.

MAKES 8 TO 10 SERVINGS

Texas-Style Beef Brisket

1 (12- to 14-lb [5.4- to 6.4-kg]) choice-grade brisket

¼ cup (60 ml) olive oil

½ cup (150 g) kosher salt

½ cup (51 g) freshly ground black pepper

Texas BBQ Sauce (page 79), warmed, for dipping

2 large, disposable aluminum pans

Hickory wood

Cooler bin large enough to contain the brisket

Place the brisket, fat side up, on a cutting board and trim the fat down to about ¼ inch (6 mm). Turn the meat over and trim away all fat pockets and silver skin from the surface of the meat. Cut away any loose or gray edges, to retain its shape and appearance.

Place the brisket in a large, disposable aluminum pan and rub it all over with the olive oil. Sprinkle the salt and pepper evenly over the meat and press firmly with your hand to adhere the spices.

Cover and refrigerate the brisket for at least 4 hours and up to overnight. One hour before you plan to cook, take the brisket out and allow it to come to room temperature.

Prepare a smoker to cook at 275°F (140°C).

Once the cooker reaches temperature, add the wood. Place the brisket, fat side down, in the smoker and cook until its internal temperature reaches 165°F (74°C), 4 to 5 hours.

Transfer the brisket to a separate large, disposable aluminum pan. Cover the pan with aluminum foil and place it in the smoker. Cook for 4 hours, or until the brisket reaches an internal temperature of 198 to 203°F (92 to 95°C) and a thermometer pushed into the meat gives little resistance.

(Continued)

Texas-Style Beef Brisket (Continued)

Remove the pan from the smoker and open the foil to vent for 10 to 15 minutes. Strain the accumulated juices of their fat and allow it to cool. Refrigerate the jus until ready to use.

Place the brisket in 2 sheets of aluminum foil and then in a clean towel; place it in an empty, dry cooler bin to rest for 2 to 3 hours.

Once the brisket has rested, transfer the reserved liquid to a medium-sized saucepan and bring it to a simmer over medium heat.

Place the brisket on a large cutting board, and using a long carving knife, slice the meat against the grain about the thickness of a number 2 pencil (about ¼ inch [6 mm] thick). You can slice it a little thicker if it is overcooked, or a little thinner if it is a bit tougher, to get the tenderness just right.

Dip each slice into the reserved jus and arrange them on a platter. Serve with BBQ sauce on the side for dipping.

These BBQ beef tacos combine two of my favorites, barbecue and tacos, in one meal! I like to slow-smoke a well-marbled chuck roast for tender, melt-in-your-mouth pulled beef and top it all off with a creamy slaw, ripe tomatoes and a shot of my sweet and spicy Texas BBQ Sauce.

MAKES 4 SERVINGS

BBQ Beef Tacos

TACO SEASONING
¼ cup (75 g) kosher salt
¼ cup (30 g) chili powder
2 tsp (5 g) smoked paprika
1 tsp granulated garlic
1 tsp onion powder
1 tsp chipotle powder
1 tsp ground cumin
1 tsp dried oregano
½ tsp freshly ground black pepper
¼ tsp cayenne pepper

1 (4-lb [1.8-g]) beef chuck roast
Olive oil
1 large onion, sliced
1 cup (240 ml) low-sodium beef broth
1 cup (240 ml) beer
½ cup (120 ml) Texas BBQ Sauce (page 79), warmed, divided
Creamy White BBQ Slaw (page 159)

TO ASSEMBLE
12 flour tortillas warmed
1 large tomato, seeded and diced

Hickory wood
Disposable aluminum half pan
Cooler bin large enough to accommodate the roast

Prepare a smoker to cook at 250°F (120°C).

Prepare the taco seasoning: In a medium-sized bowl, combine all the seasoning ingredients. Any leftovers may be stored in an airtight container for up to 6 months.

Trim the chuck roast of any excess or loose fat, then rub all sides with a thin coat of olive oil. Season the roast with an even layer of the taco seasoning and let it sit at room temperature for 30 minutes to let the rub set up.

Once the cooker reaches temperature, add the wood and place the chuck roast in the smoker. Cook for 3 hours, or until it reaches an internal temperature of 150°F (66°F).

(Continued)

BBQ Beef Tacos (Continued)

Spread the sliced onion on the bottom of a disposable aluminum half pan and top it with the chuck roast, beef broth and beer. Cover the pan with heavy-duty aluminum foil and place the pan in the smoker. Cook until the meat reaches an internal temperature of 200 to 205°F (93 to 96°C), 2 to 3 hours. Remove the pan from the smoker and open the foil to vent for 10 to 15 minutes. Strain the accumulated juices of their fat and refrigerate the jus for 2 to 3 hours, reserving the pan for later use.

Place the chuck roast in 2 sheets of aluminum foil and then in a clean towel; place it in an empty, dry cooler bin to rest for 1 to 2 hours.

When the roast has rested, transfer the reserved liquid to a medium-sized saucepan over medium heat and bring it to a simmer.

Place the roast on a large cutting board. Using 2 forks, shred the meat, discarding any fat that did not render. Place the meat back in the pan it cooked in and combine it with ¼ cup (60 ml) of the BBQ sauce and ¼ cup (60 ml) of the reserved braising liquid to moisten the meat.

Assemble the tortillas: Fill warmed flour tortillas with the shredded beef, slaw, diced tomatoes and a drizzle of BBQ sauce.

Back ribs are the beef version of baby backs. These racks remain after the butcher cuts the rib-eye roasts from the bones. Although there isn't much meat on top of the rack, it is between the bones where the delicious fatty meat is found. These ribs require a long, slow cook to reach maximum tenderness, but when you taste the smoky meat glazed with the spicy, tangy zing of the bold-flavored sauce, you'll know it's worth the wait.

MAKES ABOUT 4 SERVINGS

Sweet & Spicy Beef Back Ribs

SWEET AND SPICY RUB

¼ cup (60 g) light brown sugar

1 tbsp (4 g) dried thyme

1 tbsp (7 g) smoked paprika

1 tbsp (9 g) garlic powder

1 tbsp (19 g) kosher salt

1 tbsp (6 g) freshly ground black pepper

1 tsp cayenne pepper

½ tsp chipotle chile powder

2 racks beef back ribs (about 5 lbs [2.3 kg] total)

Olive oil

½ cup (120 ml) beef broth

2 cups (475 ml) Texas BBQ Sauce (page 79), warmed, for brushing and serving

Hickory or mesquite wood

Prepare the rub: In a small bowl, combine all the rub ingredients. Mix well and set it aside. Any leftover rub may be stored in an airtight container for up to 6 months.

Prepare a smoker to cook at 250°F (120°C).

Peel the membrane off the back side of the ribs by lifting the corner using a sharp knife, then grasping the membrane with a paper towel and pulling it off. Discard the membrane. Rub the ribs with a light coating of olive oil and season liberally on both sides with the rub. Let them sit for 30 minutes to let the rub set up.

Once the cooker reaches temperature, add the wood and place the ribs, meat side up, in the cooker directly on the grate and cook for 2½ hours. Flip the ribs and cook for 30 minutes more. Wrap each rack of ribs, meat side up, in a double layer of heavy-duty aluminum foil along with ¼ cup (60 ml) of the beef broth per rack, sealing each package tightly. Place the foil-wrapped ribs back in the smoker and cook for about an hour, or until the ribs reach an internal temperature of 205 to 208°F (96 to 98°C) and a thermometer pushed into the meat gives little resistance.

Remove the ribs from the smoker and open the foil packages to vent for 5 to 10 minutes. Discard the foil and transfer the ribs to a sheet pan. Brush the ribs with the warm sauce on both sides to coat them. Place the ribs back on the cooker for 15 minutes to set the glaze. Remove the ribs from the smoker and allow them to rest for an additional 20 minutes. Slice the ribs and arrange them on a platter. Serve with warm BBQ sauce on the side.

This award-winning chili is a perfect game day food. With the winning combination of beer, smoky bacon and spicy BBQ sauce, how can you go wrong? This dish is packed with deep, complex flavors that improve by making it a day ahead of time.

MAKES 10 TO 12 SERVINGS

Award-Winning "Triple B" Smoked Chili

1 lb (455 g) bacon, cut crosswise into ¼" (6-mm) strips

1 large onion, diced

2 jalapeño peppers, seeds and ribs removed, minced

6 cloves garlic, minced

3 lbs (1.4 kg) ground beef, 80/20

3 tbsp (22 g) ancho chile powder

2 tbsp (15 g) guajillo chile powder

2 tsp (15 g) New Mexico red chile powder

1 tbsp (7 g) ground cumin

1 tsp dried basil

½ tsp dried oregano

½ tsp dried thyme

1 tsp cayenne pepper

3 bay leaves

1 (28-oz [800-g]) can crushed tomatoes

1 (14.5-oz [429-ml]) can low-sodium chicken broth

1 (12-oz [355-ml]) bottle beer

1 (6-oz [170-g]) can tomato paste

1 cup (240 ml) Texas BBQ Sauce (page 79)

1 (15-oz [425-g]) can chili beans in sauce

1 (15-oz [425-g]) can dark red kidney beans, drained and rinsed

½ cup fresh cilantro, chopped

OPTIONAL FIXINGS

Bread bowls, for serving (optional)

Shredded cheddar cheese

Sour cream

Scallions

Pickled jalapeños

Corn chips

Oak or hickory wood

Prepare a smoker to cook at 275°F (140°C).

In a large, heavy bottomed pot or Dutch oven, cook the bacon on the stovetop over medium heat until it's browned and most of the fat is rendered, about 8 minutes. Transfer the bacon to a paper towel–lined plate and set it aside.

Pour off all but 2 tablespoons (30 ml) of the bacon grease. Add the onion, jalapeños and garlic to the pot and sauté until tender, about 6 minutes. Add the ground beef and cook until it's browned, about 5 minutes. Add the chile powders and the cumin, basil, oregano, thyme, cayenne and bay leaves. Stir well to combine them. Mix in the tomatoes, broth, beer, tomato paste and BBQ sauce. Bring it just to a boil, stirring.

Once the smoker reaches temperature, add the wood. Place the chili pot in the cooker and cook, stirring occasionally, for about an hour, or until the chili is slightly thickened. Mix in the beans, cilantro and reserved bacon and continue to cook for 10 minutes. Ladle the chili into bread bowls (if using) and top with your desired fixings to serve.

After smoking a whole brisket, I often have leftovers and I find myself looking for new ways to use them up. The addition of Texas BBQ sauce adds the sweet and spicy kick necessary to elevate this dish from good to great. Who knew that beans could be so satisfying? I swear these have become my favorite barbecue side dish, and sometimes dinner!

MAKES 12 SERVINGS

BRISKET BAKED BEANS

8 oz (225 g) bacon, diced

1 small onion, cut into small dice

1 to 2 jalapeño peppers, seeds and ribs removed, finely diced

1 lb (455 g) cooked and chopped Texas-Style Beef Brisket (page 80)

3 (28-oz [800-g]) cans pork and beans

¾ cup (175 ml) Texas BBQ Sauce (page 79)

½ cup (115 g) light brown sugar

¼ cup (60 ml) cider vinegar

2 tbsp (22 g) Dijon mustard

1 tbsp (11 g) House Rub (page 71)

Disposable aluminum half pan

Hickory wood

Prepare a smoker to cook at 250°F (120°C).

In a large saucepan, sauté the bacon over medium heat until just about cooked through but not crisp. Remove the bacon from the pan and drain it on paper towels. Divide the bacon in half.

Pour off all but ¼ cup (60 ml) of the bacon grease. Add the onion and jalapeños to the drippings in the saucepan and cook until the vegetables are tender, about 5 minutes. Add the brisket, pork and beans, BBQ sauce, brown sugar, vinegar, mustard, house rub and half of the bacon, stirring to combine them. Simmer the bean mixture for 5 minutes over medium-low heat, then transfer it to a disposable aluminum half pan.

Once the cooker reaches temperature, add the wood and place the half pan in the smoker. Cook, uncovered, for about 1½ hours, stirring after the first hour to incorporate the smoke flavor into the beans.

Stir the beans again at the 1½-hour mark and top with the remaining bacon. Cover the pan with heavy-duty aluminum foil and return the beans to the smoker. Continue to cook for an additional hour, or until the bean mixture has thickened slightly. Remove the pan from the cooker and let it rest for about 20 minutes.

Serve the beans as a hearty side dish to your barbecue, as a main dish with some crusty bread or as a topping for a baked potato.

South Carolina

MUSTARD BBQ SAUCE

If you've never had mustard BBQ sauce before, your taste buds are in for quite a revelation. This golden sauce has a savory, tart and tangy flavor with just the right amount of kick to it.

In South Carolina, an area from about Columbia to Charleston is known as the Mustard Belt, where you are more likely to find mustard-based BBQ sauce on the table, rather than the tomato-based sauces popular in other parts of the country.

Mustard-based BBQ sauce can be linked to the region's German heritage, dating back to the 1700s. These settlers brought with them their love of mustard and combined it with the Native American style of slow-cooking pork and other meats over a wood fire. Little did they know that the flavors they were creating would become such an important part of American barbecue history.

Although this sauce is traditionally served with pork barbecue, this chapter focuses on teaching you how to incorporate it into your everyday meals. You will learn how to use it to elevate salad dressings, stuffed grilled pork, smoky deviled eggs and a very grown-up, over-the-top smoked bologna.

This BBQ sauce is true Carolina gold. It's a delicious combination of mustard, brown sugar and spices that is incredible with chicken or pork. The red pepper flakes bring some background heat to this mildly sweet sauce, while the honey gently offsets the acidity of its base components.

MAKES ABOUT 2 CUPS (475 ML) SAUCE

SOUTH CAROLINA MUSTARD BBQ SAUCE

1 cup (176 g) prepared yellow mustard

½ cup (120 ml) cider vinegar

¼ cup (85 g) honey

¼ cup (60 g) packed light brown sugar

2 tsp (10 ml) Worcestershire sauce

2 tbsp (30 ml) ketchup, such as Simply Heinz

1 tsp garlic powder

1½ tsp (3 g) red pepper flakes

½ tsp salt

In a medium-sized saucepan, combine all the ingredients and cook over medium-low heat, stirring to dissolve the sugar. Lower the heat to low and simmer until it's slightly thickened, 5 to 7 minutes, stirring frequently. Let it cool, transfer it to a jar and store the sauce in the refrigerator for up to a month.

If you love Cuban sandwiches, then you are going to love this Cuban-inspired pork tenderloin. It has all the elements of the classic sandwich. After an overnight soak in the mojo marinade, the pork is slathered with the mustard BBQ sauce and stuffed with layers of ham, Swiss cheese and pickles. The meat is then seared over a charcoal grill to create an amazingly flavorful crust.

MAKES 6 TO 8 SERVINGS

Cubano Stuffed Pork Tenderloin

MARINADE

½ cup (120 ml) extra-virgin olive oil

⅔ cup (27 g) fresh cilantro leaves, chopped

Zest of 1 large orange

½ cup (120 ml) fresh orange juice

⅓ cup (120 ml) fresh lime juice

3 tbsp (18 g) fresh mint leaves, chopped

6 cloves garlic, minced

1 tsp dried oregano, or 1 tbsp (4 g) fresh

1½ tsp (4 g) ground cumin

1 tsp kosher salt, plus more to season pork roll

1 tsp freshly ground black pepper, plus more to season pork roll

2 (1-lb [455-g]) pork tenderloins, silver skin removed

South Carolina Mustard BBQ Sauce (page 95), for stuffing and drizzling

6 slices ham, sliced thinly

6 slices Swiss cheese, sliced thinly

⅔ cup (95 g) chopped bread-and-butter pickles

Prepare the marinade: In a large ziplock bag, combine the olive oil, cilantro, orange zest and juice, lime juice, mint, garlic, oregano, cumin and the salt and pepper. Add the pork tenderloin, seal the bag and toss it to coat the pork. Place the bag in a shallow baking dish and refrigerate it overnight.

Remove the pork from the marinade and discard the marinade. Pat the meat dry with paper towels.

To stuff it, cut a lengthwise slit down the center of the tenderloin, two-thirds of the way through the meat. Open the halves, laying the tenderloin flat. Place the tenderloin between 2 sheets of plastic wrap and pound it to ½-inch (1.3-cm) thickness, using a meat mallet. Evenly spread about 2 tablespoons (30 ml) of the BBQ sauce per loin over the pork. Layer the meat with the ham, Swiss cheese and pickles. Roll the layers up, starting with the long side, and secure it with butcher's twine at 2-inch (5-cm) intervals. Season the meat with salt and pepper.

Set up a charcoal grill for 2-zone cooking. Light a charcoal chimney, and when the edges of the charcoal at the top of the chimney begin to ash over, dump the pile of hot coals onto 1 side of the grill to form your hot side (direct cooking), leaving the other side empty to form your cool side (indirect cooking), forming 2 zones.

(Continued)

Cut a lengthwise slit down the center of the tenderloin ⅔ of the way through the meat

Using a meat mallet, pound the meat to ½-inch (1.3-cm) thickness

Spread the BBQ sauce evenly over the pork

Layer the pork with pickles

Layer the pork with swiss cheese

Layer the pork with the ham slices

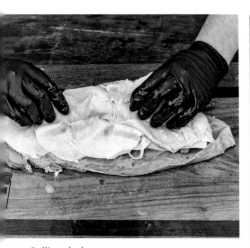

Rolling the layers up

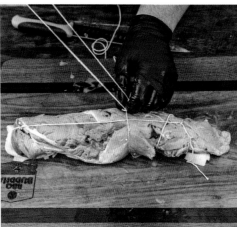

Secure the meat with butcher's twine

Searing the meat on the grill

Once the charcoal is ready, place the tenderloin directly over the hot coals and put the lid back on to cover it. Cook for 5 minutes. Flip the tenderloin and cook for another 5 minutes. Now, move the meat to the indirect heat zone. Place the lid back on the grill to cover the tenderloin and continue to cook until the pork reaches an internal temperature of 150°F (66°F), 15 to 20 minutes.

Remove the pork from the grill and let it rest for about 10 minutes, loosely covered with foil. Remove the string and cut the stuffed tenderloin into 1-inch (2.5-cm) slices. Arrange them on a platter and drizzle them with BBQ sauce to serve.

This smoked bologna recipe is far from the bologna of your youth. A 3-pound (1.4-kg) chub is scored and slathered with Mustard BBQ Sauce, then coated with sweet BBQ rub before hitting the smoke. Slice the bologna to make sandwiches or cube and serve it with the mustard BBQ sauce on the side for dipping.

MAKES ABOUT 20 SERVINGS

Smoked Bologna

1 (3-lb [1.4-kg]) chub bologna

¼ cup (60 ml) South Carolina Mustard BBQ Sauce (page 95), plus more for dipping

¼ cup (44 g) House Rub (page 71)

Hickory or pecan wood

Prepare a smoker to cook at 250°F (120°C).

Using a sharp knife, score the bologna about ⅛ inch (3 mm) deep in a diamond pattern on all sides of the meat.

Brush the bologna chub with the BBQ sauce and season it with the house rub, opening the slits slightly with your fingers to get the rub into the cuts you just made.

Once the smoker reaches temperature, add the wood and place the bologna on the grate in the cooker. Smoke for about 3 hours, or until the meat develops a nice mahogany color.

Remove the meat from the smoker and let it rest for 10 minutes. Slice, serve and enjoy!

This is a classic steakhouse-style spinach salad with a barbecue twist. Crisp bacon, mushrooms, onions and sliced smoked eggs are mixed with fresh baby spinach that has been tossed with the warm, tangy BBQ vinaigrette. This hearty salad makes for a great side dish or a light dinner.

MAKES 4 SERVINGS

Spinach Salad with Warm Bacon Mustard BBQ Vinaigrette

4 hard-boiled large eggs, peeled and chilled

VINAIGRETTE
¼ cup (60 ml) white wine vinegar
⅓ cup (80 ml) South Carolina Mustard BBQ Sauce (page 95)
¼ cup (85 g) honey

2 slices thick-cut bacon, chopped
1 cup (70 g) sliced cremini mushrooms
1 large shallot, minced
1 clove garlic, minced
Salt and freshly ground black pepper

TO ASSEMBLE
1 (10-oz [280-g]) bag baby spinach
4 slices thick-cut bacon, cooked and crumbled
1 cup (110 g) shredded Swiss cheese

Pecan wood

Smoke the eggs: Prepare a smoker to cook at 200°F (90°C).

Once the smoker reaches temperature, add the wood. Place the eggs on a baking rack directly on the grate and cook for about 30 minutes. Remove the eggs from the cooker and chill them until ready to use. Slice the eggs just before serving.

Prepare the vinaigrette: In a small bowl, whisk together the vinegar, BBQ sauce and honey. Set it aside.

In a sauté pan, cook the chopped bacon over medium heat, stirring occasionally, until most of the fat is rendered and the bacon is just starting to crisp. Add the mushrooms to the pan and cook for about 5 minutes. Stir in the shallot and garlic and cook until they're tender and fragrant, about 2 minutes.

Lower the heat to low and stir in the vinaigrette. Season with salt and pepper to taste and continue to cook until it's warmed through, about 2 minutes. Remove the pan from the heat and set it aside.

Assemble the salad: Place the spinach in a large serving bowl and toss it with the warm vinaigrette mixture. Garnish the salad with the sliced smoked eggs, crumbled bacon and shredded Swiss cheese to serve.

While I was growing up, my mom's deviled eggs were my favorite appetizer. Lucky for me, they made it to every family cookout and were always served on our holiday table. These were luscious, creamy, eggy bites with just a hint of mustard. When I set out to make my own version, I knew that I wanted to amp up that tangy mustard flavor. By smoking the eggs and adding this savory mustard BBQ sauce rather than plain old mustard I was able to achieve that pop of flavor I was looking for while keeping it balanced with the smoky pork. You can make these your own by including any number of unique BBQ toppings, such as bacon, brisket or chunks of diced smoked bologna.

MAKES 24 SERVINGS

Smoked Deviled Eggs with Shredded Pork

Nonstick spray

12 hard-boiled large eggs, peeled

⅓ cup (75 g) mayonnaise

1 tbsp (15 ml) South Carolina Mustard BBQ Sauce (page 95), plus more for garnish

1 tsp hot sauce, such as sriracha

Smoked paprika

1¼ cups (188 g) Slow-Smoked Pork Shoulder (page 34), heated and shredded

Minced chives

Hickory or pecan wood

Smoke the eggs: Prepare a smoker to cook at 200°F (90°C). Spray a baking rack with nonstick spray.

Once the cooker reaches temperature, add the wood and place the eggs on the prepared baking rack, then set the rack directly on the grate in the smoker. Cook for about 30 minutes. Remove the eggs from the cooker and chill them until ready to use.

Assemble the deviled eggs: Cut the eggs in half lengthwise. Cut a thin slice off the bottom of each half, so they won't tip over when plated. Scoop out the yolks and place them and the egg white trimmings in a food processor.

Add the mayonnaise, BBQ sauce and hot sauce and process to a thick puree. You can add a touch more mayonnaise, if you like a creamier consistency.

Spoon the mixture back into the egg white halves. Top the eggs with a dusting of smoked paprika, shredded pork and minced chives. Place the eggs in a shallow container, cover and refrigerate them until ready to serve, then garnish them with a drizzle of BBQ sauce.

This is a great recipe to have in your arsenal of barbecue side dishes. It is my version of the traditional southern potato salad. The flavors in this dish really come together with the addition of smoky bacon and tangy mustard BBQ sauce. I like to top it off with sliced green onions for an added pop of flavor and color.

MAKES 6 TO 8 SERVINGS

Bacon Potato Salad with Creamy Mustard BBQ Dressing

2½ lbs (1.1 kg) red potatoes, rinsed and cut into ¾" (2-cm) pieces

2 tsp (12 g) salt, plus more for seasoning

DRESSING

¾ cup (175 g) mayonnaise, such as Duke's

¼ cup (60 ml) South Carolina Mustard BBQ Sauce (page 95)

1 tbsp (15 ml) cider vinegar

1 lb (455 g) bacon, cooked and crumbled

2 ribs celery, cut into small dice

3 scallions, thinly sliced

½ small red onion, diced

5 hard-boiled eggs, peeled and diced

Freshly ground black pepper

Place the potatoes in a large pot with 2 teaspoons (12 g) of salt and completely cover them with water. Bring it to a boil over medium-high heat, then lower the heat to medium and cook for 15 to 20 minutes, or until the potatoes are fork-tender.

Drain the potatoes in a colander and transfer them to a large bowl. Allow them to cool for 15 minutes.

Prepare the dressing: In a large bowl, whisk together the mayonnaise, BBQ sauce and vinegar.

Add the potatoes, bacon, celery, scallions, red onion and eggs to the dressing and gently toss to combine them.

Season to taste with salt and pepper. Cover and refrigerate the salad until ready to serve.

Tangy Peach
BBQ SAUCE

Our annual Fourth of July cookout was quickly approaching, and I began searching for some new flavors to add to the menu. My guests had become accustomed to the variety of sauces that I served alongside our smoky feast every year, and I wanted to give them something new and different.

As my mind began to wander, I thought of the many distinctive BBQ sauces that I had tried on southern road trips. I kept coming back to a roadside barbecue shack in Georgia that served an outstanding peach BBQ sauce at the table.

On my quest to re-create this delicious sauce, I tried over a dozen different versions, achieving the most consistent results by using canned peaches mixed with peach preserves. That combination yielded a sauce with just the right amount of tanginess and a subtly sweet peach flavor.

In this chapter, you will learn what it means to plank cheese on the grill (page 121), the secret to becoming your neighborhood wing king (page 118) and how to prepare Competition-Style Smoked Chicken Thighs (page 112), using this inspirational sauce that pairs well with pork and poultry.

Butter, onion and brown sugar provide the base of this thick, orange-colored sauce that bounces tangy tastes off the fruity sweetness of a subtle peach flavor. This is a versatile sauce that you can use in competitions as well as your own backyard, with great results.

NOTE: If you prefer to use fresh peaches, substitute 2 cups (500 g) of peach puree (from about five large peaches) for the peach preserves and canned peaches.

MAKES ABOUT 5 CUPS (1.1 L) SAUCE

PEACH BBQ SAUCE

1¼ cups (400 g) peach preserves

1 (15-oz [425-g]) can sliced peaches, drained

4 tbsp (55 g) unsalted butter

½ small onion, diced

1½ cups (355 ml) ketchup, such as Simply Heinz

½ cup (115 g) light brown sugar

½ cup (120 ml) cider vinegar

½ cup (120 ml) water

2 tbsp (30 ml) Worcestershire sauce

2 tbsp (22 g) Dijon mustard

1 tsp salt

2 tsp (4 g) freshly ground black pepper

¼ tsp ground thyme

1 tsp granulated garlic

2 tsp (10 ml) hot sauce, such as Crystal

In a food processor, combine the peach preserves and sliced peaches. Blend them to a puree.

In a medium-sized saucepan, melt the butter over medium-high heat and sauté the onion until it's soft but not browned, 3 to 4 minutes. Stir in the peach puree, ketchup, brown sugar, vinegar, water, Worcestershire, Dijon, salt, pepper, thyme, granulated garlic and hot sauce. Lower the heat to medium-low and simmer until it's slightly thickened, 15 to 20 minutes, stirring frequently. Let the sauce cool, transfer it to a jar and store it in the refrigerator for up to 3 weeks.

In competition barbecue, you are judged on appearance, taste and tenderness. It is common for competitors to brine their chicken before smoking it, as this helps to retain moisture and flavor as it cooks, thus improving tenderness. This tangy peach BBQ sauce can certainly help you gain points for appearance and flavor, whether you are cooking in your backyard or on the competition trail. It gives you that perfect sweet heat bite, with a subtle peach finish that is sure to win over family, friends and maybe even a barbecue judge or two.

MAKES 12 SERVINGS

COMPETITION-STYLE SMOKED CHICKEN THIGHS

CHICKEN RUB

1 cup (200 g) cane sugar

½ cup (150 g) kosher salt

¼ cup (28 g) smoked paprika

2 tbsp (13 g) freshly ground black pepper

1½ tsp (4 g) onion powder

1½ tsp (4 g) granulated garlic

1 tsp ground thyme

1½ tsp (7 g) celery salt

1 tsp cayenne pepper

12 chicken thighs

Poultry Brine (page 156)

1 cup (225 g) margarine, divided

2 cups (475 ml) Peach BBQ Sauce (page 111)

Large disposable aluminum pan

Apple or sugar maple wood

Prepare the rub: In a medium-sized bowl, combine all the rub ingredients and set it aside. Leftover rub may be stored in an airtight container for up to 6 months.

Trim the fat from the thighs and cut away any loose hanging skin to make them all about the same size. They should look like little rectangular pillows. Using a meat tenderizer, such as a Jaccard, pierce holes in the chicken skin by placing the unit over the meat and pressing down. Repeat until you have pierced both sides of the thighs.

Three hours before you plan to cook, place the chicken thighs in a large, lidded container and pour the brine over the meat. Cover the container and refrigerate it for 2 hours.

Remove the chicken from the brine and rinse well. Pat the thighs dry with a paper towel and refrigerate them for 1 hour.

Prepare a smoker to cook at 275°F (140°C). Fit a sheet pan with a baking rack.

Sprinkle an even layer of the chicken rub all over the chicken thighs. Place the thighs, bone side down, in a large, disposable aluminum pan and top each thigh with a pat of margarine.

(Continued)

Competition-Style Smoked Chicken Thighs (Continued)

Once the cooker reaches temperature, add the wood.

Place the pan in the smoker and cook for 1 hour. Lightly re-season the top of the thighs with the rub and wrap the pan with aluminum foil. Return the pan to the cooker until the chicken reaches an internal temperature of 180°F (82°C), 30 to 40 minutes. Remove the pan from the cooker and open the foil to vent for 1 to 2 minutes.

In a medium-sized saucepan over medium heat, stir the BBQ sauce until it's warmed. Using tongs or gloved hands, submerge each thigh in the warmed sauce. Place the thighs on the rack-topped baking sheet to drain any excess sauce. Place the pan in the smoker and cook for 15 to 20 minutes to set the glaze. Remove the chicken from the smoker and let it rest for 5 minutes before serving.

A rack of pork, also known as a pork rib roast, is an impressive cut of meat that includes the pork loin and back ribs. Using this method, the meat will slowly come up to temperature as it cooks in the smoker before it is seared over hot coals, giving it a golden-brown crust. Glazing the meat with the tangy peach BBQ sauce adds yet another layer of flavor and complements the smoke and spice. Serving the roast whole makes for a beautiful presentation at your next dinner party or holiday meal.

MAKES 8 SERVINGS

Reverse-Seared Center-Cut Rack of Pork

1 (5- to 6-lb [2.3- to 2.7-kg]) bone-in pork loin roast with chine bone removed
Pork Brine (page 135)
Olive oil
House Rub (page 71)
Peach BBQ Sauce (page 111), warmed, for brushing and dipping
Apple or cherry wood

Trim the pork loin roast by removing the silver skin and any loose hanging fat. Peel away the membrane from the back side of the ribs and French the bones. (To French is to strip the meat away from the bone of a rib or a chop to cleanly expose the bone.) Alternatively, you can ask your butcher to do this for you.

Place the roast in a 2½-gallon (9.5-L) ziplock bag and pour the brine over it. Refrigerate the roast for at least 6 hours or up to overnight.

Prepare a smoker to cook at 250°F (120°C).

Remove the roast from the brine and discard the brine. Rinse the roast and pat it dry with paper towels. Coat the meat with a thin layer of olive oil. This will help the rub stick to the meat. Season liberally with the house rub and let it sit for 30 minutes to allow the rub to set up.

Once the cooker reaches temperature, add the wood and place the roast in the smoker. Cook for 2 to 2½ hours, or until the roast reaches an internal temperature of 140°F (60°C).

(Continued)

Reverse-Seared Center-Cut Rack of Pork (Continued)

Set up a charcoal grill for 2-zone cooking. Light a charcoal chimney, and when the edges of the charcoal at the top of the chimney begin to ash over, dump the pile of hot coals onto 1 side of the grill to form your hot side (direct cooking), leaving the other side empty to form your cool side (indirect cooking), forming 2 zones.

Once the grill reaches temperature, place the roast, meat side down, on the grate directly over the hot coals and sear for 6 minutes. Flip the roast over and sear for 6 minutes more. Move the pork loin to the indirect side of the grill and brush it with the warm BBQ sauce. Place the lid back on the grill and cook for 5 minutes to set the glaze.

Transfer the pork loin from the grill to a sheet pan and tent it loosely with foil. Let the meat rest for about 20 minutes. You can present the roast whole to your guests and then cut in between the bones to create each portion. Arrange the portions on a platter to serve with more BBQ sauce for dipping.

These smoked and grilled chicken wings are the best of both worlds. You really can have it all. Tender smoked chicken is infused with great barbecue flavor, and the skin, crisp from the grill, is glazed with sweet and spicy BBQ sauce.

MAKES 6 TO 8 SERVINGS

Smoked & Grilled Chicken Wings

WING RUB

½ cup (115 g) light brown sugar

½ cup (28 g) paprika

1 tbsp (13 g) cane sugar

1 tbsp (18 g) salt

1 tbsp (6 g) freshly ground black pepper

1 tbsp (8 g) chili powder

1 tbsp (9 g) granulated garlic

1 tbsp (7 g) onion powder

1 tsp dried oregano

1 tsp cayenne pepper

5 lbs (2.3 kg) chicken wings, flats and drums

Peach BBQ Sauce (page 111), warmed, for serving

Hickory or sugar maple wood

Prepare the rub: In a medium-size bowl, combine all the rub ingredients and set it aside. Leftover rub may be stored in an airtight container for up to 6 months.

Prepare a smoker to cook at 275°F (140°C). Fit a sheet pan with a baking rack.

Season the wings with the wing rub and place them on the rack-topped sheet pan.

Once the cooker reaches temperature, add the wood. Place the pan in the smoker and cook for 1 hour. Flip the wings and cook until they reach an internal temperature of 165°F (74°C), about 45 minutes to an hour more.

While the wings are smoking, fire up a charcoal grill to cook at around 375°F (190°C), direct cooking method. To set up your grill for direct cooking light up a charcoal chimney, and when the edges of the charcoal at the top of the chimney begin to ash over, dump the hot coals into the grill. Using long-handled metal tongs, even out the charcoal to create even heat distribution throughout.

Transfer the cooked wings to the grill and place them over direct heat. Grill for about 2 minutes per side to crisp up the skin. Remove the wings from the grill and toss them with the warmed peach BBQ sauce to serve.

The next time you are having company over, try making this easy yet impressive-looking appetizer on the grill. Start by brushing the cheese with the BBQ sauce prior to grilling, and as the wood plank begins to char, it will release a nice smoke flavor that will permeate the food as it cooks.

MAKES 4 SERVINGS

Planked Camembert with Prosciutto-Wrapped Grilled Peaches

8 thin slices prosciutto, halved lengthwise

2 medium-sized peaches, halved, pitted and cut into 8 wedges each

Salt and freshly ground black pepper

Olive oil

1 small wheel Camembert or Brie cheese, scored

Peach BBQ Sauce (page 111), for brushing and dipping

Grilled bread, for serving

Cedar grilling plank

Set up a charcoal grill for 2-zone cooking. Light a charcoal chimney, and when the edges of the charcoal at the top of the chimney begin to ash over, dump the pile of hot coals onto 1 side of the grill to form your hot side (direct cooking), leaving the other side empty to form your cool side (indirect cooking), forming 2 zones.

Lay out the prosciutto slices on a work surface. Set a peach wedge at the edge of each slice and season with salt and pepper to taste. Roll up the prosciutto to enclose the peaches and brush them with a thin coating of olive oil. Set them aside until you are ready to cook.

Once the grill reaches temperature, char the plank: Place it directly over the fire and grill until the plank is singed on both sides, 1 to 2 minutes per side. Set it aside and let it cool.

Grill the prosciutto-wrapped peaches over the direct heat zone, turning occasionally, until the prosciutto is browned and crisp, about 4 minutes. Transfer the prosciutto-wrapped peaches from the grill to a platter and set it aside.

Place the cheese on the plank and brush the top with some of the BBQ sauce. Lay the plank in the center of the grill and close the lid. Cook for about 5 minutes, then place the prosciutto-wrapped peaches around the cheese wheel on the plank. Brush the prosciutto with the BBQ sauce and close the lid. Cook for 4 to 5 minutes or until the sides of the cheese are soft and beginning to bulge. Transfer the plank to a heatproof platter and serve the peaches with grilled bread and more BBQ sauce for dipping.

These are one-bite "shots" that are filled with smoked pork, creamy cheese and a hint of spice. The sweet and tangy peach glaze cuts through this decadent appetizer, culminating in a rich, balanced bite of barbecue heaven.

MAKES ABOUT 30 SERVINGS

Pig Shots

1 lb (455 g) smoked andouille or kielbasa sausage

1 lb (455 g) thick-cut bacon, cut in half lengthwise

8 oz (225 g) cream cheese at room temperature

1 tbsp (11 g) House Rub (page 71), plus more for dusting

1 cup (225 g) packed light brown sugar

Peach BBQ Sauce (page 111), warmed, for brushing and dipping

Wooden toothpicks, for securing bacon

Disposable aluminum half pan

Hickory or cherry wood chunks

Soak the toothpicks in a shallow bowl of water for 1 hour before cooking.

Prepare a smoker to cook at 275°F (140°C).

Cut the sausage into ½-inch (1.3-cm) slices.

Wrap a ½ strip of bacon around each sausage slice and secure it with a toothpick to form a shot glass.

In a small bowl, mix the cream cheese with the tablespoon (11 g) of house rub. Pipe or spoon the cream cheese into each pig shot, leaving a little room at the top.

Top each shot with 1½ teaspoons (7 g) of brown sugar and a dusting of the house rub. Place the pig shots in a disposable aluminum half pan.

Once the cooker reaches temperature, add the wood and place the pan on the smoker. Cook for 1½ to 2 hours, or until the bacon is just starting to crisp up. Brush each shot with the warm BBQ sauce and return the pan to the cooker for another 10 minutes to set the glaze.

Remove the pan from the smoker and allow the shots to rest for 5 minutes, as the filling will be hot. Serve with a side of BBQ sauce for dipping.

Cherry Bourbon
BBQ SAUCE

When it came time for me to develop a new competition sauce, I wanted something with rich, complex flavors: a sauce that would dance on the judge's palate just long enough to stand out without overwhelming the meat.

Previously, I had been working on a cherry BBQ sauce that I really liked but felt needed something more to elevate it from good to great. When thinking of flavor profiles that complement barbecue, it finally hit me: bourbon!

Bourbon is traditionally aged in charred oak barrels, during which time it develops a smoky, caramel flavor. It's a natural spirit that is minimally processed, and the sharp flavors in the bourbon offset the tartness of the cherries.

Barbecue and bourbon are the perfect match. These two iconic symbols of the American South showcase time-honored traditions of the men and women who work hard every day, honing their crafts for the rest of the world to enjoy.

In this chapter, I will teach you how to turn ordinary chicken legs into sweet and smoky glazed lollipops (page 128), prepare award-winning St. Louis–Style Ribs (page 131), wow your guests with a smoked holiday ham (page 136) and much more. So grab an apron and let's get cooking!

My approach to sauce-making is to find the simplest route to the best flavor—that's why I chose to use cherry juice as opposed to whole cherries. I think it helps provide a more consistent end product, as whole fruits tend to vary in ripeness and sweetness. This brilliant red sauce, bursting with lively flavors that are sweet, tart, smoky and slightly spicy, is a fine complement to burgers, chicken and pork, especially ribs.

MAKES ABOUT 3 CUPS (710 ML) SAUCE

Cherry Bourbon BBQ Sauce

1 cup (240 ml) unsweetened cherry juice

⅓ cup (115 g) honey

1 cup (240 ml) ketchup, such as Simply Heinz

⅓ cup (115 g) light brown sugar

¼ cup (64 g) tomato paste

¼ cup (60 ml) cider vinegar

3 tbsp (45 ml) bourbon

2 tsp (10 ml) hot sauce, such as Crystal

1½ tsp (9 g) kosher salt

1 tsp freshly ground black pepper

1 tsp granulated garlic

1 tsp onion powder

½ tsp dry mustard

½ tsp celery salt

In a medium-sized saucepan, combine all the ingredients and bring it to a gentle boil over medium heat, stirring to dissolve the sugar. Lower the heat to low and simmer until the sauce is slightly thickened, 20 to 25 minutes, stirring it frequently. Let it cool, transfer the sauce to a jar and store it in the refrigerator for up to a month.

This is a cool way to turn ordinary chicken legs into a fun and delicious appetizer. To do it, you'll need a sharp knife and a pair of kitchen shears. The meat is cut loose from the small end and pushed down, creating a "lollipop" look. The leg bone is left clean and creates the "stick." This presentation is sure to wow your guests!

MAKES 12 SERVINGS

Smoked Chicken Lollipops

12 chicken drumsticks
Chicken Rub (page 112)
½ cup (112 g) unsalted butter
Cherry Bourbon BBQ Sauce (page 127), warmed, for glazing
Disposable aluminum half pan
Hickory wood

Prepare a smoker to cook at 300°F (150°C).

Using a sharp knife or a pair of kitchen shears, make a cut completely around the lower part of the leg just below the knuckle, cutting through the skin and tendons. Push the meat down to the large end and pull the remaining skin and cartilage off the knuckle to leave the bone clean.

Season the legs with the chicken rub and let them sit out for 30 minutes, then wrap the exposed bones with a piece of aluminum foil. This will prevent them from becoming dark during cooking.

While the smoker is heating, place the butter in a disposable aluminum half pan and set it inside the cooker to melt. The butter will add flavor and moisture to the cooking process, but it doesn't need to cover the chicken.

Once the cooker reaches temperature, add the wood and place the chicken legs in the pan of butter, with the bones sticking straight up. Cook for 2 hours, or until the chicken reaches an internal temperature of 170°F (77°C).

Line a sheet pan with aluminum foil and fit a baking rack on the pan. Next, remove the aluminum foil from the chicken bones and, using tongs or a gloved hand, dip each entire lollipop into the warm BBQ sauce. Arrange the legs on the rack-topped sheet pan so that the bones are sticking straight up. Place the pan in the smoker and cook until the chicken reaches 175°F (79°C) and the glaze is set, about 30 minutes.

Remove the chicken from the cooker and let them rest for 10 minutes, uncovered. Arrange the legs on a platter to serve.

St. Louis–style ribs are popular in the world of competitive barbecue because they are meatier, have a higher fat content and are more uniform in shape than baby back ribs. A slab is almost a perfect rectangle, which makes for even cooking all the way through. Removing the membrane from the back of the ribs not only helps the rub and smoke flavors penetrate the meat, it also helps you create a meltingly tender bite.

MAKES ABOUT 8 SERVINGS

St. Louis–Style Ribs

2 (2½-lb [1.1-kg]) slabs St. Louis–cut pork ribs

¼ cup (44 g) prepared yellow mustard

½ cup (88 g) House Rub (page 71), plus more for dusting

Apple juice, for spritzing

½ cup (170 g) honey

1 cup (225 g) packed light brown sugar

¼ cup (60 ml) hot sauce, such as Crystal

4 tbsp (56 g) unsalted butter, melted

1 cup (240 ml) Cherry Bourbon BBQ Sauce (page 127), warmed

Hickory or cherry wood

Wooden toothpick, for testing doneness

Prepare a smoker to cook at 250°F (120°C).

Remove the membrane from the back of the ribs and trim away any excess fat. Remove the end bones from each slab to square them up. Apply a thin coat of mustard to each side. Sprinkle on an even layer of the house rub to both sides of the ribs. Let them sit for 30 minutes to let the rub set up.

Once the cooker reaches temperature, add the wood.

Place the ribs on the smoker and cook for 2½ hours, spritzing with apple juice every 30 minutes. Lay out 2 sheets of heavy-duty aluminum foil. Layer half of the honey, brown sugar, hot sauce and butter on each foil. Lightly dust these with some more of the rub and spritz them with apple juice. Place each slab of the ribs, meat side down, on each honey mixture–topped sheet of foil and wrap up the foil packages tightly. Place the wrapped ribs back on the pit and continue to cook for about an hour, then check the ribs for doneness by opening the packages and pushing a toothpick into the meat. It should go in and out easily. Continue to cook to your desired tenderness. Once the ribs are done, remove them from the smoker and open the foil to vent for about 15 minutes. This will prevent the ribs from further cooking. Remove them from the foil and transfer the ribs to a sheet pan.

Combine ¼ cup (60 ml) of the juices from the foil with the BBQ sauce and brush it onto both sides of the ribs to glaze. Place the ribs back on the smoker and cook for 15 to 20 minutes to set the glaze. Remove the ribs from the cooker and allow them to rest for 5 minutes. Slice the ribs individually and arrange them on a platter to serve.

If you are looking for an extra-special appetizer or entrée for your next gathering, this is it. Crab-stuffed bacon-wrapped shrimp are easy to assemble ahead of time and refrigerate until you are ready to grill. I recommend partially cooking the thin-cut bacon, leaving it flexible enough to wrap around the shrimp, otherwise the shrimp will be overcooked before the bacon browns.

MAKES 18 TO 20 SERVINGS

CRAB-STUFFED BACON-WRAPPED SHRIMP

Nonstick spray

8 oz (225 g) cream cheese at room temperature

4 oz (115 g) lump crabmeat

2 cloves garlic, minced

1 tbsp (6 g) thinly sliced scallion

1 tbsp (15 ml) hot sauce, such as Crystal

2 lbs (905 g) classic cut bacon

2 lbs (905 g) jumbo shrimp (16 to 20 count), peeled and deveined, tail on

House Rub (page 71)

Cherry Bourbon BBQ Sauce (page 127), warmed, for brushing

Wooden toothpicks, for securing bacon

Soak the toothpicks in a shallow bowl of water for 1 hour before cooking.

Preheat the oven to 400°F (200°C). Line 2 sheet pans with foil and spray the foil with nonstick spray. Additionally, spray a baking rack with nonstick spray and set it aside.

In a medium-sized bowl, combine cream cheese, crabmeat, garlic, scallion and hot sauce. Mix well, cover and set it aside

Place the bacon on the prepared sheet pans. Once the oven reaches temperature, place the pans in the oven and cook for about 10 minutes. Drain the bacon on a paper towel–lined plate.

Set up a charcoal grill for 2-zone cooking. Light a charcoal chimney, and when the edges of the charcoal at the top of the chimney begin to ash over, dump the pile of hot coals onto 1 side of the grill to form your hot side (direct cooking), leaving the other side empty to form your cool side (indirect cooking), forming 2 zones.

Fill each shrimp with 1 teaspoon of the crab mixture. Wrap it with a slice of bacon and secure it with a toothpick. Dust the shrimp with the house rub and arrange them on the prepared baking rack. Place the rack on the indirect heat side of the grill and cook for 4 minutes. Flip and cook until the shrimp turn pink and the bacon begins to crisp, about 4 minutes. Brush them with the BBQ sauce and remove them from the grill.

Arrange the shrimp on a platter to serve.

Soaking lean cuts in a brining solution helps retain moisture and helps tenderize the meat. A delightful honey garlic rub underscores the caramel tones of the sauce in this tender and flavorful pork loin dish.

MAKES ABOUT 6 SERVINGS

BRINED & SMOKED PORK LOIN

HONEY GARLIC RUB

⅓ cup (58 g) granulated honey

2 tbsp (18 g) granulated garlic

1 tbsp (7 g) paprika

1 tsp chipotle chile powder

1 tbsp (8 g) chili powder

1 tbsp (18 g) sea salt

1 tsp freshly ground black pepper

1 tbsp (7 g) onion powder

2 tbsp (11 g) Italian seasoning

1 tsp ground thyme

1 tsp celery salt

PORK BRINE

6 cups (1.4 L) cold water

2 cups (475 ml) apple juice

½ cup (115 g) packed light brown sugar

¼ cup (75 g) kosher salt

2 tbsp (10 g) black peppercorns

2 sprigs thyme

½ bunch parsley

3 cloves garlic, sliced

1 (2½-lb [1.1-kg]) boneless center-cut pork loin

1 tbsp (15 ml) olive oil

Cherry Bourbon BBQ Sauce (page 127), warmed

Apple or peach wood

Prepare the rub: In a medium-sized bowl, combine all rub ingredients and set it aside. Leftover rub may be stored in an airtight container for up to 6 months.

Prepare the brine: In a medium-sized bowl, mix together all the brine ingredients until the brown sugar and salt have dissolved. Refrigerate the brine for at least 4 hours, or until ready to use, preferably overnight. Just before using, strain the brine through a fine-mesh strainer. Place the pork loin in a heavy ziplock bag and add enough of the cold brine to cover the meat entirely. Press out as much air as possible and seal the bag. Refrigerate it for 12 to 24 hours, turning occasionally.

Prepare your smoker to cook at 250°F (120°C).

Remove the pork from the brine and discard the brine. Rinse the roast well and pat it dry with paper towels. Coat the pork with a thin layer of olive oil. This will help the rub stick to the meat. Liberally coat the meat with the honey garlic rub and let it sit for 30 minutes to allow the rub to set up.

Once the cooker reaches temperature, add the wood and place the roast in the smoker. Cook until the pork reaches an internal temperature of 145°F (63°C), about 2 hours. Remove the pork from the smoker and brush it generously with the warm BBQ sauce. Return the loin to the cooker to set the glaze, about 10 to 15 minutes.

Remove the pork from the smoker and cover it loosely with foil. Let the meat rest for 20 minutes. Slice and arrange the pork on a platter to serve with extra BBQ sauce for dipping.

Are you looking to cook something different on the smoker for the holidays? If you are anything like me, the answer is yes! I am constantly looking for reasons to fire up my cooker, and this double-smoked ham fits the bill. Here, a fully cooked spiral ham is coated with rub, slow-smoked and glazed for an easy yet impressive addition to your holiday table.

MAKES ABOUT 15 SERVINGS

Double-Smoked Ham

1 (8- to 10-lb [3.6- to 4-kg]) fully cooked spiral-sliced ham

House Rub (page 71)

Cherry Bourbon BBQ Sauce (page 127), warmed, for brushing and serving

Hickory or pecan wood

Prepare a smoker to cook at 275°F (140°C).

Season the ham all over with the house rub, getting some in between the slices for added flavor, and let it sit out for 30 minutes.

Once the cooker reaches temperature, add the wood and place the ham in a small pan on the grate in the smoker. Cook for 1½ hours, then brush it with the BBQ sauce. Return the ham to the smoker and continue to cook until the ham reaches an internal temperature of 140°F (60°C), 30 to 40 minutes.

Remove the ham from the smoker and let it rest, loosely covered with foil, for 15 minutes.

To carve the ham: Turn the ham on its bottom so that the meat is facing up. Using a long knife, cut around the bone. Then, cut through the natural breaks in the ham where the fat lies to separate the meat.

Arrange the ham slices on a platter with a bowl of BBQ sauce to serve.

Asian
BBQ SAUCE

I love the many styles and regions of American barbecue and all its accompanying sauces. However, I must admit, I had always wanted to learn the secret to creating a great Asian BBQ sauce, like the kind that you would get at your favorite Chinese restaurant, but with a deeper, richer, umami flavor.

As I put together the basic structure for this recipe, I let my affection for Cantonese cuisine guide the way. I knew immediately that hoisin sauce would be the perfect base for this sauce.

Hoisin is a thick, sweet and salty sauce made from fermented soybean paste. It is typically used in stir-fries, as a marinade and to glaze grilled meats and fish. It is sometimes referred to as Chinese BBQ sauce.

I added a few ingredients to the hoisin (ketchup, sugar, vinegar and garlic) that are commonly added to American BBQ sauces, but I wanted to balance it out with some distinctly Asian flavors, such as grated fresh ginger, Chinese five-spice powder and sesame oil. Soy sauce and black garlic were then added to naturally enhance the savory or umami flavor of this sauce.

Let the recipes in this chapter inspire you to re-create Chinese takeout classics, such as Asian BBQ Beef Skewers (page 150), BBQ Sticky Ribs (page 149) and BBQ Pork Meatballs (page 142), while creating new favorites, such as Smoked Pork Belly Bites (page 146) and Cedar Planked Salmon (page 145).

This dark, clingy sauce is great for coating meat in layers of flavor or as a dunking sauce. Fermented black garlic gives this sauce a complex, sweet and savory molasses-like richness with tangy garlic undertones. Grated fresh ginger brightens the sauce, providing a counterpoint to the garlic.

NOTE: Black garlic is available at many specialty grocers, although I prefer to get mine shipped from Black Garlic Market in Pensacola, Florida, https://www.facebook.com/blackgarlic196/.

MAKES ABOUT 2 CUPS (475 ML) SAUCE

Asian BBQ Sauce

½ cup (120 ml) all-natural hoisin sauce, such as Joyce Chen

¼ cup (60 ml) dry sherry

¼ cup (60 ml) soy sauce

¼ cup (50 g) sugar

2 tbsp (10 g) grated fresh ginger

⅔ cup (160 ml) ketchup, such as Simply Heinz

¼ cup (60 ml) seasoned rice vinegar

2 cloves garlic, minced

2 cloves black garlic, minced

¼ tsp Chinese five-spice powder

2 green onions, minced

2 tsp (10 ml) sesame oil

In a medium-sized saucepan, combine all the ingredients, except the sesame oil. Simmer over medium-low heat for 8 to 10 minutes, or until the sauce has slightly thickened. Remove the pan from the heat and stir in the sesame oil. Let the sauce cool, transfer it to a jar and store it in the refrigerator for up to 2 weeks.

If you love meatballs as much as I do, then you must try my Asian BBQ–inspired version. The sauce punctuates the full flavor of these easy-to-make pork meatballs. Serve them on toothpicks as an appetizer, on lettuce wraps for a snack or with your favorite rice and vegetables as an entrée.

MAKES ABOUT 30 SERVINGS

BBQ Pork Meatballs

Nonstick spray
2 lbs (905 g) ground pork
2 tsp (10 ml) sesame oil
1 cup (60 g) panko bread crumbs
½ tsp ground ginger
2 large eggs
1 tbsp (10 g) minced garlic
½ cup (50 g) thinly sliced scallion
Asian BBQ Sauce (page 141), warmed, for dipping
Toasted sesame seeds

Set up a charcoal grill for 2-zone cooking. Light a charcoal chimney, and when the edges of the charcoal at the top of the chimney begin to ash over, dump the pile of hot coals onto 1 side of the grill to form your hot side (direct cooking), leaving the other side empty to form your cool side (indirect cooking), forming 2 zones.

Lightly spray a baking rack with nonstick spray.

In a large bowl, combine the ground pork, sesame oil, bread crumbs, ginger, eggs, garlic and scallion and mix thoroughly.

Form the meat into 1-ounce (28-g) balls and place them on the prepared rack. This will make it easier to move the meatballs to and from the smoker.

Once the grill reaches temperature, place the rack on the grate over the indirect heat side and cover it with the grill lid.

Cook the meatballs until they reach an internal temperature of 160°F (71°C), 12 to 15 minutes. Remove the rack from the cooker and use a pair of tongs to dip each meatball into the warm BBQ sauce.

Arrange the meatballs on a platter and garnish them with toasted sesame seeds to serve.

Grilling the salmon on a cedar plank results in a moist and subtly smoky fish. I like to add sake or beer to the water prior to soaking the planks for additional flavor. The thick finishing sauce adheres to the fish, glazing it in a savory garlic that augments the smoke flavor. For an impressive presentation, serve the salmon on the plank that it was grilled on.

MAKES 4 SERVINGS

Cedar Planked Salmon

2 cups (475 ml) sake or beer, to soak cedar plank (optional)

MARINADE
½ cup (115 g) light brown sugar
¼ cup (60 ml) soy sauce
2 cloves garlic, minced
1 tsp sesame oil

1 (1½-lb [680-g]) salmon fillet
Asian BBQ Sauce (page 141), warmed, for brushing
1 tbsp (6 g) thinly sliced scallion
Cedar plank

Soak the plank in cool water (add the sake or beer, if using) for 1 hour, weighing the wood down with a heavy object to keep it submerged.

Prepare the marinade: In a small bowl, stir together the brown sugar, soy sauce, garlic and sesame oil.

Place the salmon in a ziplock bag and pour in the marinade to cover it. Seal the bag and toss it to coat the fish. Refrigerate it for 1 hour.

Set up a charcoal grill for 2-zone cooking. Light a charcoal chimney, and when the edges of the charcoal at the top of the chimney begin to ash over, dump the pile of hot coals onto 1 side of the grill to form your hot side (direct cooking), leaving the other side empty to form your cool side (indirect cooking), forming 2 zones.

Remove the salmon from the marinade and discard the marinade. Place the salmon, skin side down, on the plank. Transfer the plank to the grill and place it on the direct heat zone. Close the lid and cook for 10 minutes. Brush the salmon with the BBQ sauce and move the plank to the indirect heat side. Cover the grill and continue to cook until the internal temperature of the fish reaches 135 to 140°F (57 to 60°C), 6 to 8 minutes, depending on the thickness of your salmon. Remove the plank from the grill and allow the fish to rest for 5 minutes. Transfer the plank to a platter and garnish the fish with scallions to serve.

Pork belly cooked in the style of beef burnt ends has grown increasingly popular in recent years, and for good reason. It is the same cut of meat that bacon comes from, so it is loaded with flavor and takes a lot less time to produce than its beef counterpart. These bite-sized pieces of smoky, sweet and tender pork belly are the perfect finger food for your next party or tailgate.

MAKES 16 TO 20 SERVINGS

Smoked Pork Belly Bites

Nonstick spray

1 (4- to 5-lb [1.8- to 2.3-kg]) slab uncured pork belly, skin removed

Honey Garlic Rub (page 135)

½ cup (120 ml) apple juice

Asian BBQ Sauce (page 141), warmed

2 tbsp (28 g) honey

Apple wood

Disposable aluminum pan

Prepare a smoker to cook at 250°F (120°C). Lightly spray a baking rack with nonstick spray.

Using a sharp knife, cut the pork belly into 2-inch (5-cm) squares.

Season the pork all over with the honey garlic rub and let it sit out for 30 minutes. Place the pork cubes on the prepared baking rack. This will make it easier to move the meat to and from the smoker.

Once the cooker reaches temperature, add the wood and place the rack on the grate in the smoker. Cook until the pork reaches an internal temperature of 165°F (74°C), about 2½ hours.

Remove the pork belly from the cooker and place it in a disposable aluminum pan. Pour the apple juice around the meat, then wrap the pan tightly with heavy-duty aluminum foil and return it to the smoker. Cook until the pork reaches an internal temperature of 200°F (93°C), about 1 hour.

Remove the pork belly from the smoker and open the foil to vent for 10 minutes. Reserve 2 tablespoons (30 ml) of the braising liquid and discard the rest.

In a large bowl, combine the BBQ sauce, honey and reserved braising liquid. Place the pork cubes into the mixture and toss to coat them. Return the pork to the disposable aluminum pan and place it back on the smoker to cook for 20 to 30 minutes to set the sauce. Remove the pork bites from the smoker and let them rest for 10 minutes. Arrange them on a platter to serve.

These better-than-takeout Asian BBQ spareribs are next level. Seasoning them with the Chinese five-spice powder and marinating them overnight in the savory BBQ sauce helps develop the flavors in the meat. The ribs are basted and slow-cooked until tender, then quickly seared until charred, glazed and sticky.

MAKES 2 TO 4 SERVINGS

BBQ Sticky Ribs

1 (2-lb [905-g]) slab St. Louis–style spareribs

1 tbsp (6 g) Chinese five-spice powder

1½ cups (355 ml) Asian BBQ Sauce (page 141), divided, for basting and serving

Sprinkle the Chinese five-spice powder over the ribs and rub it into the meat until it's evenly coated. Cut the ribs into individual portions and place them in a large ziplock plastic bag. Pour in 1 cup (240 ml) of the BBQ sauce to coat the ribs. Seal the bag and refrigerate the ribs for 6 to 8 hours or up to overnight.

Set up a charcoal grill for 2-zone cooking. Light a charcoal chimney, and when the edges of the charcoal at the top of the chimney begin to ash over, dump the pile of hot coals onto 1 side of the grill to form your hot side (direct cooking), leaving the other side empty to form your cool side (indirect cooking), forming 2 zones.

Remove the ribs from the marinade and discard the marinade. Place the ribs on the indirect heat side of the grill; cover and cook for 1 hour. Baste the ribs with the reserved ½ cup (120 ml) of BBQ sauce, flip and baste again. Continue to cook until the ribs are tender, charred and sticky, 15 to 20 minutes.

Transfer the ribs from the grill to a platter and let them rest for 10 minutes. Serve with a side of BBQ sauce.

You can use either skirt or flank steak for this recipe, but I prefer to use skirt because it is a well-marbled cut with a higher fat content. Marinate the beef skewers before grilling them over the direct heat side of your charcoal grill, for maximum flavor and tenderness. Keep an eye on these skewers as they tend to cook quickly. Brush them with the BBQ sauce to caramelize on the meat in the last few minutes of cooking.

MAKES ABOUT 15 SERVINGS (2 PER SERVING)

Asian BBQ Beef Skewers

MARINADE

⅓ cup (80 ml) olive oil

⅓ cup (80 ml) soy sauce

¼ cup (85 g) honey

2 cloves garlic, minced

1 tbsp (15 ml) rice vinegar

1 (1" [2.5-cm]) piece fresh ginger, sliced

½ tsp red pepper flakes

½ tsp freshly ground black pepper

1½- to 2-lbs (680- to 905-g) skirt steak, silver skin removed, cut into 6 x 1½" (15 x 4–cm) pieces

Asian BBQ Sauce (page 141), warmed, for brushing

Sesame seeds

Wooden skewers

Place the wooden skewers in a shallow dish and cover them with water to soak for 1 hour prior to cooking.

Prepare the marinade: In a medium-sized bowl, stir together the olive oil, soy sauce, honey, garlic, vinegar, ginger, red pepper flakes and black pepper.

Place the steak strips in a large ziplock bag and cover them with the marinade. Seal the bag and refrigerate it for 1½ to 2 hours.

Set up a charcoal grill for 2-zone cooking. Light a charcoal chimney, and when the edges of the charcoal at the top of the chimney begin to ash over, dump the pile of hot coals onto 1 side of the grill to form your hot side (direct cooking), leaving the other side empty to form your cool side (indirect cooking), forming 2 zones.

Remove the meat from the marinade and discard the marinade; thread the steak strips onto the skewers.

Working in batches, if necessary, place the skewers on the direct heat side of the grill and cook for about 3 minutes per side. Move the skewers to the indirect heat side of the grill and brush them with the warm BBQ sauce. Close the lid on the grill and continue to cook for 1 to 2 minutes.

Remove the skewers from the grill and arrange them on a platter to serve. Garnish with sesame seeds.

Alabama

WHITE BBQ SAUCE

Robert "Big Bob" Gibson of Big Bob Gibson Bar-B-Q restaurant in Decatur, Alabama, is credited with creating white sauce back in 1925. Although it may not be what you envision when you think of traditional barbecue sauce, this rich and flavorful sauce is a true southern classic.

The first time I tried Alabama white sauce was at an unassuming mom-and-pop restaurant in Alabama on a long drive to compete at the World Food Championships. One thing that stood out about this white sauce with flecks of pepper was its versatility. This tangy mayonnaise-based condiment, which was traditionally used to dress chickens, is also used to marinate, baste or dip various smoked or grilled meats.

As with many BBQ sauces, you want to apply this only in the final minutes of your grilling or smoking. It is best used as a finishing sauce, otherwise it may break down and separate from being heated too long.

In this chapter, you will discover an assortment of uses for white BBQ sauce. It can serve as a vegetable dip or a highly seasoned mayonnaise in salads or coleslaw, and traditionally smoked chicken halves get dunked in this sauce for an incredible finish.

This creamy white sauce is tangy and peppery with just a hint of sweetness. While the classic pairing of this north Alabama sauce is with chicken, you can also use it to add refreshing notes to a variety of grilled or smoked foods, including poultry, fish, pork and vegetables.

MAKES ABOUT 3½ CUPS (828 ML) SAUCE

Alabama White BBQ Sauce

2 cups (250 g) mayonnaise, such as Duke's

⅔ cup (160 ml) cider vinegar

½ cup (120 ml) apple juice

2 tsp (8 g) Creole mustard

2 tsp (10 g) prepared horseradish

2 tsp (4 g) freshly ground black pepper

2 tsp (10 ml) fresh lemon juice

1 tsp salt

½ tsp cayenne pepper

In a large bowl, whisk together all the ingredients. Cover and refrigerate it for at least 30 minutes before using. Transfer any unused sauce to a jar and refrigerate it for up to 2 weeks.

Are you ready to try perfectly smoked chicken dunked in the legendary Alabama white sauce? This combination has stood the test of time. Splitting the chicken in half not only creates more surface area for the smoke to penetrate and "season" the meat, it promotes even cooking. You can cut the chicken yourself or ask your butcher to do it for you.

MAKES 4 SERVINGS

Smoked Chicken Halves

POULTRY BRINE

1 gal (3.8 L) warm water (about 110°F [43°C])

½ cup (150 g) kosher salt

⅔ cup (150 g) packed light brown sugar

1 large onion, sliced

1 bunch thyme

1 bunch parsley

1 tbsp (5 g) black peppercorns

1 bay leaf

1 (3½- to 4½-lb [1.6- to 2-kg]) chicken

Chicken Rub (page 112)

Alabama White BBQ Sauce (page 155), for brushing

Apple wood

Prepare the brine: In a large, lidded container, whisk together the warm water, salt and brown sugar until the sugar and salt are dissolved. Add the onion, thyme, parsley, peppercorns and bay leaf. Refrigerate it until ready to use. The brine can be made up to 4 days ahead of time. Strain it before use.

Cut the chicken in half: Position it so that its back is facing up. Using a pair of kitchen shears, cut along both sides of the backbone to remove it. You should be able to open the chicken up like a book. Starting at the neck, cut down the center line to separate the halves. Trim away any excess fat or loose hanging skin.

Brine the chicken: Place the chicken halves in a large, lidded container and pour the brine over the meat. Cover the container and refrigerate it for 2 to 3 hours.

Prepare a smoker to cook at 300°F (150°C).

Remove the chicken from the container and discard the brine. Rinse the chicken and pat it dry with paper towels. Season the chicken halves with the chicken rub and let them sit out for 30 minutes to let the rub set up.

Once the cooker reaches temperature, add the wood and place the chicken halves on the grate in the smoker. Cook until the chicken reaches an internal temperature of 180°F (82°C) in the thickest part of the thigh, 1½ to 2 hours. Remove the chicken from the smoker and let it rest for 10 minutes.

Just before serving, brush the chicken generously with the BBQ sauce. If you are feeling adventurous, you can try doing it as they do at Big Bob Gibson's and dunk the chicken in a vat of sauce to coat it!

I like to use Alabama White BBQ Sauce (page 155) as the dressing for my coleslaw. It adds a sweet and tangy flavor that's hard to beat when served on a barbecued chicken or pork sandwich. This recipe is easily doubled to take along to your next potluck or cookout.

MAKES ABOUT 6 SERVINGS

CREAMY WHITE BBQ SLAW

1 (1-lb [455-g]) package coleslaw mix

½ cup (120 ml) Alabama White BBQ Sauce (page 155)

2 tbsp (28 g) mayonnaise, such as Duke's

¼ cup (40 g) thinly sliced sweet onion, such as Vidalia

Salt

Ground white pepper

In a medium-sized bowl, combine the coleslaw mix, BBQ sauce, mayonnaise and onion. Season with salt and white pepper to taste. Cover and refrigerate the slaw until ready to serve.

This flavor-packed pasta salad is a great side dish for your next cookout or tailgate. You can also add a protein, such as pulled chicken, to turn it into a hearty lunch. Whenever I make this dish, my guests always come back for a second helping, and sometimes a third!

MAKES 12 TO 15 SERVINGS

BBQ Pasta Salad

1 cup (240 ml) Alabama White BBQ sauce (page 155)

¼ cup (60 g) mayonnaise, such as Duke's

2 tsp (5 g) chili powder

1 lb (455 g) macaroni, such as tricolor rotini, cooked and drained

1 (15-oz [425-g]) can black beans, drained and rinsed

1½ cups (225 g) grilled corn kernels (cut from 2 to 3 ears after grilling)

1 red onion, grilled and diced

1 cup (115 g) shredded sharp cheddar cheese

1 pint (178 g) sweet grape tomatoes, cut in half

1 avocado, peeled, pitted and cubed

1 bunch scallions, sliced thinly

In a large bowl, stir together BBQ sauce, mayonnaise and chili powder. Add the pasta and stir to coat it. Add the black beans, corn, red onion, cheddar cheese and tomatoes and mix well. Cover and refrigerate the salad.

Garnish the salad with cubed avocado and sliced scallions, to serve.

This is a great southern lunch counter dish and the perfect way to use up any leftover smoked chicken you may have. By shredding or pulling the chicken, rather than chopping it, you are increasing the surface area that the sauce will cover, thus creating a creamy, smoky, peppery bite. I like to serve it over crisp greens with salty bacon, sharp cheddar cheese and slices of sweet, crisp Gala apple.

MAKES 4 SERVINGS

Smoked Chicken Salad Plate

CHICKEN SALAD

1 cup (240 ml) Alabama White BBQ sauce (page 155)

¼ cup (60 g) mayonnaise, such as Duke's

2 ribs celery, diced

1 lb (455 g) leftover pulled chicken from Beer Can Chicken (page 48) or Smoked Chicken Halves (page 156)

Salt and freshly ground black pepper

1 large head romaine lettuce, chopped

8 slices bacon, cooked and crumbled

1 cup (115 g) shredded sharp cheddar cheese

1 bunch scallions, sliced thinly

2 Gala apples, cored and sliced thinly

Baguette bread, sliced and grilled

Prepare the chicken salad: In a medium-sized bowl, whisk together the BBQ sauce and mayonnaise. Add the celery and chicken and stir to combine them. Season with salt and pepper to taste.

Assemble the plates: Divide the chopped romaine equally among 4 plates. Place a 4-ounce (115-g) scoop of the chicken salad in the center of each and garnish it with bacon, cheddar cheese, scallions, sliced apples and grilled bread, to serve.

Giving vegetables a quick marinade before they hit the grill prevents them from drying out and helps create a sweet caramelized char on the outside. The next time you are entertaining, set out a grilled vegetable platter with a bowl of white peppery BBQ sauce for dipping and watch your guests devour it in no time.

MAKES ABOUT 12 SERVINGS

GRILLED VEGETABLE CRUDITÉS

MARINADE

½ cup (120 ml) olive oil

¼ cup (85 g) honey

2 tbsp (30 ml) balsamic vinegar

2 tsp (2 g) dried oregano

1 tsp granulated garlic

1 tsp onion powder

¼ tsp dried thyme

Salt and freshly ground black pepper

1 lb (455 g) asparagus, trimmed

6 small carrots, peeled then cut in half lengthwise

3 variously colored bell peppers, seeded and cut into 1" (2.5-cm) strips

1 bunch scallions, trimmed

2 large portobello mushroom caps, cut into 1" (2.5-cm) strips

Nonstick spray

Alabama White BBQ sauce (page 155), for dipping

Prepare the marinade: In a medium-sized bowl whisk together the olive oil, honey, vinegar, oregano, granulated garlic, onion powder and thyme. Season with salt and pepper to taste.

Place the vegetables in a large ziplock bag and pour in the marinade to cover them. Seal the bag and turn it to coat the vegetables. Marinate the vegetables at room temperature for 1½ to 2 hours.

Light a charcoal chimney, and when the edges of the charcoal at the top of the chimney begin to ash over, dump the pile of hot coals onto 1 side of the grill to form your hot side (direct cooking), leaving the other side empty to form your cool side (indirect cooking), forming 2 zones. Spray a baking rack with nonstick spray.

Arrange the vegetables on the prepared rack and place the rack on the direct heat side of the grill to cook for 2 to 3 minutes, then flip the vegetables and cook for another 2 to 3 minutes. Move the rack to the indirect heat side of the grill, close the lid and cook until they're tender, about 6 minutes.

Remove the vegetables from the grill and let them cool for 5 minutes. Arrange them on a platter and serve with a bowl of BBQ sauce for dipping.

Acknowledgments

My wife, Kelly Sheehan, for being such an amazing partner in life, business and love. I am truly blessed to have you by my side on this journey.

My mom, Lucille, for nurturing my love of the culinary arts and teaching me that anything is possible if you are willing to work for it. My sister, Kristine, for always believing in me.

Glen Vandervort, my right-hand man and teammate on the competition trail, for taking time out of his busy schedule to help me, again.

To my publisher, Will Kiester and my editor, Marissa Giambelluca, for giving me the opportunity to write this book. To the entire staff at Page Street Publishing, for bringing this book to life and guiding me through the process. Ken Goodman, for capturing the soul of each dish with his beautiful photographs.

Tim O'Keefe, for jumping in at the last minute to help me get through the editing process.

Bill Gillespie, for his inspiration and encouragement, as well as a very important introduction.

Stewart Goldstein, for being an expert butcher, true friend and advocate.

Tim Citrone for helping more times than I can count and especially for cooking with me for the photo shoot.

Kell and Janet Phelps at the *National Barbecue News*, for giving me the opportunity to contribute to their award-winning publication.

Bob Trudnak, for writing the foreword to this book.

Lisa Jo Goetter and everyone at BBQ Guru, for their continued support.

Mark Joseph Kelly, for his dedication in helping build our BBQ Buddha brand.

Love to my Cravings family, for making this journey that much sweeter: Jan, Stu, Kate, Sheri and Faye.

Stuart Kramer, "Just three words!" BUY MY BOOK!

David Malek at Gunter Wilhelm, for the amazing cutlery and cookware.

John Prokop at Cuttingboards2go.com, for the beautiful, fine wood cutting boards.

About the Author

Ray Sheehan is the founder and owner of BBQ Buddha, an international award-winning line of healthy-minded BBQ sauces and rubs. He is also the pitmaster for the BBQ Buddha Competition team and a certified Kansas City Barbeque Society judge. Ray spends his time running the day-to-day operations of the business, but his true passion is creating award-winning BBQ products. His sauces have won numerous awards, including Scovie Awards, the National Barbecue & Grilling Association's Awards of Excellence, the International Artisan Flavor Awards (The Flaves) and the World Hot Sauce Awards—Barbecue Sauce Divisional Champion. A chef by trade, Ray has been in the food business for over 25 years. Since 2017 he has been a contributor to the *National Barbecue News* magazine, providing recipes, articles and product reviews. Ray has appeared on *PA Live!* WBRE-NBC, *Barbecue Nation with JT*, WKRE-Portland, Oregon, *Small Bites* with Derek Timm & Donato Marino and *The Pit Life* BBQ podcast. He has been featured in *Tailgater Magazine*, *Edible Jersey* magazine, *New Jersey Monthly* magazine, *Industry Magazine*, the *Asbury Park Press* and the *Coaster* newspaper. He lives in New Egypt, New Jersey, with his wife, Kelly, son Raymond, and dogs, Serena and Sammy.

For more information about Ray and his award-winning products, please visit www.bbqbuddha.com.

Index